The Little Stuff
Matters Most

The Little Stuff
Matters Most

50 Rules from 50 Years of
Trying to Make a Living

Bernie Brillstein
WITH DAVID RENSIN
ILLUSTRATIONS BY DAVID SIPRESS

GOTHAM BOOKS

GOTHAM BOOKS
Published by Penguin Group (USA) Inc.
375 Hudson Street, New York, New York 10014, U.S.A.
Penguin Group (Canada), 10 Alcorn Avenue, Toronto, Ontario, Canada M4V 3B2 (a division
of Pearson Penguin Canada Inc.); Penguin Books Ltd, 80 Strand, London WC2R 0RL, Eng-
land; Penguin Ireland, 25 St Stephen's Green, Dublin 2, Ireland (a division of Penguin Books
Ltd); Penguin Group (Australia), 250 Camberwell Road, Camberwell, Victoria 3124, Australia
(a division of Pearson Australia Group Pty Ltd); Penguin Books India Pvt Ltd, 11 Community
Centre, Panchsheel Park, New Delhi—110 017, India; Penguin Group (NZ), Cnr Airborne and
Rosedale Roads, Albany, Auckland, New Zealand (a division of Pearson New England Ltd);
Penguin Books (South Africa) (Pty) Ltd, 24 Sturdee Avenue, Rosebank, Johannesburg 2196,
South Africa

Penguin Books Ltd, Registered Offices: 80 Strand, London WC2R 0RL, England

Published by Gotham Books, a division of Penguin Group (USA) Inc.

First American printing, September 2004
10 9 8 7 6 5 4 3 2 1

Gotham Books and the skyscraper logo are trademarks of Penguin Group (USA) Inc.

LIBRARY OF CONGRESS CATALOGING-IN-PUBLICATION DATA
Brillstein, Bernie, 1931–
    The little stuff matters most : 50 rules from 50 years of trying to make a living / by Bernie
Brillstein with David Rensin ; illustrations by David Sipress.
    p. cm.
    ISBN 1-59240-079-5 (hardcover : alk. paper)
    1. Success in business—Anecdotes. 2. Conduct of life—Anecdotes. 3. Motion picture
producers and directors—United States—Anecdotes. 4. Theatrical agents—United States—
Anecdotes. I. Rensin, David. II. Title.
    HF5386.B835 2004
    650.1—dc22   2004007024

Printed in the United States of America
Set in Galliard with Bodega Serif
Designed by Sabrina Bowers

This book is printed on acid-free paper. ∞

In a world where celebrity equals talent, and where make-believe is called reality, it is most important to have real love, truth, and stability in your life.

◆

To my beautiful wife, Carrie, and my wonderful children: Leigh and Abe; David; Nick, Claire, and Alden; Michael; and Kate. Thanks for giving me so much love and fun. And to our wonder dog, Lucy: We couldn't forget you.

◆

Thanks, as usual, to David Rensin for always getting it right.

Contents

Introduction

W HEN *THE NEW YORK TIMES* reviewed my 1999 memoir, *Where Did I Go Right?: You're No One in Hollywood Unless Someone Wants You Dead,* the book was described as "unmistakably Brillstein: loud, astute, crude, alternately self-aggrandizing and self-deprecating, and full of stories."

And, by the way, they loved it.

Much has been said about me since I started in the mail-room at the William Morris Agency in New York fifty years ago and worked my way up and out as an agent, consultant, TV packager, movie and television producer, motion picture studio head, and talent manager. Some of it is even true. But I think producer Lynda Obst, writing in the *Los Angeles Times,* got to the heart of me when she declared, "Bernie Brillstein is a *way of being* in work. It is rapture in work."

We've all got to make a living. What's the point if you don't love your work?

Because I love what I do, I've tried to be smart about it. I've paid attention to the lessons of tradition and kept my eyes on the new. I've celebrated my victories and made the best of my mistakes. I've solved problems with common sense instead of fancy theories.

I guess I did all right. I've personally guided the careers of Jim Henson; John Belushi; Gilda Radner; Dan Aykroyd; *Saturday Night Live* creator Lorne Michaels; John Larroquette; Martin Short; Rob Lowe; Wayne Brady; my first client, Norm Crosby; writer/producer Alan Zweibel—and many others.

In 1992, I cofounded Brillstein-Grey Entertainment with Brad Grey, who now owns the company and has taken it to new heights. Among the many clients are Brad Pitt, Jennifer Aniston, Adam Sandler, and Nicolas Cage.

The company also produced shows like *Just Shoot Me, ALF, NewsRadio, Politically Incorrect, Mr. Show*, and the current sensation, *The Sopranos.*

Along the way, I had the idea for *Hee Haw,* helped get *The Blues Brothers* and *Ghostbusters* made (and *Dangerous Liaisons*, among others, when I ran Lorimar Pictures), got my own star on Hollywood Boulevard's Walk of Fame, won an Emmy, and got to know Jiminy Glick personally. Go figure.

Not only have I managed to survive and prosper, but I'm happy. My greatest achievement.

But I could never have done any of it—and kept it going— if I hadn't remembered this: *In business as in life, the little stuff matters most.*

Outcomes rarely turn on grand gestures, high-flying concepts, or the art of the deal—and more often on whether you've sent someone a thank-you note.

It's the truth.

Success is almost always about the basics. You stay in the game by playing by the right rules. Manners. Smarts. Open eyes. Counterintuitive thinking. A lot of knowledge about what you do. To me, truth comes through life experience. Common sense. The wisdom of trusted friends.

But how do you get that knowledge? I always looked to the past, to people who'd already learned the lessons. I got what I had to know to survive from the street in an era when one still had the luxury of time to absorb and grow. Now everything is too fast-paced, too corporate, and this bedrock of wisdom is being lost. It shouldn't be.

I try to do my part to perpetuate tradition. For instance, at my company I'm now the guy the kids—and I call everyone "kid," even if they're older than I am—come to. My office door is always open, and rarely a day goes by without someone wandering in to ask for advice or to talk about a situation. I've lived long enough, watched the wheel of life turn often, and paid attention. I've seen the same act again and again, no matter how much it looks like it's changed. That's probably why—not because I look like Santa Claus—that people always ask, "What should I do, Bernie?"

That's fine, as long as no one wants to sit on my lap.

When someone selling a movie script, or themselves as an actor, or their service as an executive producer on a TV show, asks me, "What's the right price?"—a question that you hear no matter what business you're in—I tell them the right price is whatever they're willing to pay you, and whatever you're willing to take. How much do you need the job? How much is your mortgage? How badly do they want you?

I remember a bright, promising kid who was so focused on what someone else in the office was doing and earning that his own work had suffered. Suddenly, he thought he might get fired. I told him to take a seat on the couch, made sure he had a glass of water, and said: "One big problem with business today is that everyone wants to know what the other guy makes, what he's up to. You should mind your *own* business. By 'minding' I mean paying attention. You can't do business if you don't focus. You can't make it big if you keep looking over your shoulder at the guy behind you, thinking, 'He's getting awfully close,' or at the guy ahead of you, thinking, 'Why don't I have what he has, do what he does?' Worry about yourself. I don't mean you should be a selfish ass; I mean that too many people want to be someone else: They want the other guy's job, his clothes, his car, his girlfriend, his salary. They want to be him. But if you want to be someone else, you can't be you. And if you're not you—as scary as that might seem at times—you have no chance."

So a competitor tried to stab you in the back? Learn not to make drama out of an incident and let your enemy bury himself.

It's not always about the bottom line, but what's at the bottom of your heart.

Do something for the thrill of it all, not for the thrill of having it all.

Understand that there's a difference between hot and good.

Have an opinion—even if it's wrong.

Remember that winners make the tough calls and deliver bad news quickly.

God helps Himself, but you've got to ask (for that raise).

When your time has come, success will find you.

And for goodness' sake, turn off the pager and cell phone once in a while, meet friends face-to-face, don't talk about work, and laugh as much as possible.

It's not always strictly business, either. Once someone wrote to me asking: "I recently became well known in movies. I am also single. Suddenly, members of the opposite sex are very interested in me. How can I tell if they actually like me for me, or whether it's just the money and fame they like?"

My answer: "Who cares? Enjoy it!"

Okay, there was more: "Let me tell you something: You could have no money, and you'd still have no way of knowing if they love you for your body, your face, or just you.

"Take the love you can get as you get it. What do you have to examine it for? If you're a movie star, and someone wants to go to bed with you and you like them? Fine. If they want to take you to dinner? Fine. If you don't like them, then don't go out. How are you going to figure out what someone's real intentions are when they don't know what their real intentions are? You have to try it before you buy it.

"Of course, if you're a big movie star, the likelihood is that everyone will want to say they've been with you. So yes— you're probably going to get more charlatans in the mix. If your last motion picture price was $20 million and a gaffer comes on to you, who knows? Maybe you just turn him on, and he turns you on. What's wrong with that?"

◆

My advice is based only on what's worked for me, so of course you're asking why you should believe it will work for you.

All I can offer as proof is that I'm still around after all these years. I've been right more often than wrong, and that's when people start to think that maybe you actually know something.

That's why the publisher asked me to write this book.

To be perfectly honest, I hesitated at first. I read biographies, not self-help books. I don't subscribe to esoteric management theories that not only guarantee to make you rich, powerful, and smarter than anyone else in the room, but throw in a way to lose weight while still eating all you want. Imagine that.

I should probably tell you I wrote this book because I'm a smart guy, and that the publisher made me such a wonderful offer that, being so savvy, I gave myself some very important advice: *Don't be an idiot. Take the dough.*

The truth is a little more complicated. They made me such a wonderful offer that I thought, *Don't be an idiot. Take the dough. But make absolutely sure you really believe in what you're doing.*

You wouldn't listen to my advice if I didn't follow it myself.

Frankly, I was a little leery of doing this book because I've never imagined myself as some business guru. Also, the reaction to my memoir was so fantastic that I figured I should quit while I was ahead. (Another good bit of advice, though I can't claim to have thought of it first. Whoever did, quit, and hasn't been heard from since.)

But then I remembered how often my show business con-

temporaries, mailroom trainees, college students, a
called or wrote to tell me they highlight pages in my
and refer to it when they need a second opinion. Nice. ~~~ ~~~~
first book is nearly five hundred pages long. Who could carry it
around everywhere? It made more sense to put my best big
ideas into a small volume, a "Pocket Bernie" if you will, that
could easily fit into anyone's . . . well, pocket or bag. No more
heavy lifting.

That sold me.

Who could resist performing a public service?

◆

The Little Stuff Matters Most is my collection of in-the-
trenches common sense so fundamental that, with all that's
been built atop it, it might seem uncommon. It distills fifty
years of accumulated experience, insight, and instinct—in
both business and life—into one slim volume of big ideas
that's easy to carry everywhere and to consult anytime you
think a dose of clearheaded advice is required. There is no
magic here, just unfailing honesty and unflinching directness.

In other words, this book is the closest you can come to
having a personal manager on call at all times, without having
to part with 15 percent of your paycheck.

Let me put it in classic Hollywood-speak: *The Little Stuff
Matters Most* is like "zesty, bite-sized chunks of *Don't Sweat the
Small Stuff*, *The Sayings of Chairman Mao*, *Harvey Penick's Little Red Book on Golf*, and *The Elements of Style* all floating in a
bowl of chicken soup for the businessman's soul." Okay. It
helps to have a sense of humor.

Please don't look at this as a rule book, but as a collection of suggestions. Guidelines. There are no rules for the rules. Everyone has different rules. Your personality has to go with your rules. There are twenty guys and gals in every business who have made it because they followed their own rules. It's not that complicated. Only brain surgery is brain surgery.

If you don't learn anything—though I think you will—at least you'll get a laugh and be entertained, so it won't be a total loss.

◆

Now that we're getting to the end of this preamble, I want to make sure I've been absolutely clear about one thing: *The Little Stuff Matters Most* is not a book of secrets. There's no Zen, no art of, no formula, no mystical philosophy; there are no three rules, seven habits, or ten steps. There are no tedious worksheets or personal diaries to keep. No daily affirmations. No seminars to attend—yet. You won't feel worse about yourself if you don't follow the program exactly because there is no program.

I don't pull punches though, so a thick skin helps.

There's also no test at the end of this book. The real test is living day to day. Being happy. The idea is to be able to get through it all and still come out ahead. The only way to do that is by helping yourself. I can point you in the right direction, but in the end you have to rely on your own instincts and wherever they lead you—or you're screwed.

And best of all, you can still eat all you want.

The Little Stuff
Matters Most

The Little Stuff Matters Most

PAY ATTENTION TO THE little things.

Brush your teeth before you kiss your wife.

Say "Good morning" to everyone in your office when you walk in. Have a joke.

Always have clean fingernails. It's the first thing people see.

Howard Stern said a really smart thing once: "Who are you going to hire—a guy who walks in wearing a clean sweater, a clean shirt, shined-up shoes, and pressed pants, or the guy who comes in with dreadlocks, a baseball hat on backwards, and pants that are too big?"

Call people to check in. Not only when you need something, but to say, "Hello, how are ya. How do you feel? What about the ball game last night?"

If someone is needy, take their call even if you can't or don't want to do anything for them. Make them feel like they're still in the human race.

Be polite in your car. In the restaurant. Everywhere.

ure you know people's names. If you don't, intro-
elf first; they'll tell you.

..... a date, call up and say you had a good time even if
you didn't. Don't promise to call again if you won't.

There's nothing wrong with a hug. Just don't be a pain in
the ass about it.

If more people had manners in their business life, they
would fare better. That's why your parents teach you manners
in the first place—not so you can have separate rules of behavior out of the house. At home you're expected to be on time, to
consider other people's feelings, to say please, thank you, and
you're welcome. It's the Golden Rule. Answer or return every
phone call. Keep your office door open. Mine is. I don't like to
be interrupted but if someone wants to walk in badly enough,
I want to talk to them. You can call my style outdated but I
think it's just smart management technique because it's not a
technique at all. I'd rather wander the halls and find out what's
going on instead of hiding in my office collecting information.

There's a saying in politics that "all politics is local," meaning that you'd better pay attention to the people who actually
voted you into office because they can just as easily vote you
out. In business, the votes are cast not only by your boss, but
by your coworkers and, most important, by the client. Take
the William Morris Agency. Say what you will about the place,
but it's been in business 106 years. Why? They do the little
things that are important to clients, like show up at perfor-
mances. They put a face on their business.

Some people think manners have no place in business
because it's all about wielding power and destroying your ene-

mies. If you don't care, you're more in control, right? Bullshit. Politeness and power are not mutually exclusive. In fact, being polite enhances power because people realize that when you've stopped being nice it means the situation is serious—and watch out. We all have to break someone's balls sometimes, but does that mean we can't send flowers or write a thank-you note? What does it take? If you're too busy to put pen to paper, dictate it to your assistant, who will have the good fortune to learn from you that the little stuff matters most.

You also can't be too loyal. Be there in the good times and the bad times, and always be honest. If someone gets fired, don't take him out of your Rolodex. Keep him in, call him at his next job—or just call him at home to see how he is.

The people I care about know it, but it's not good enough to just say so. I call to congratulate them on an opening weekend, for working hard, or just for finishing a project—long before anyone knows if it will be successful. Too often I hear, "Bernie, God bless you. Besides my wife, you're the only person I've heard from."

You don't really need an excuse to write or call or send a gift. In the end, you can do it for no reason at all.

First, Put Yourself in the Game

IF YOU'RE NOT ON the playing field, you'll never discover if the game is for you, if you have an instinct for it, or if you're any good at it. Too many people imagine what they might become but are so afraid of failing—or worse, being caught in something they can't get out of—that they stay on the sidelines. Everyone who goes for an interview is scared. Get over it. Go in with the idea of testing yourself.

But first you have to get in the game.

Come to the job interview with the basics covered: clean, well-dressed, good manners. You need to know something about the business you want to be in. You probably also need a college degree; in Hollywood these days it takes a sheepskin just to get into a mailroom.

Next you have to communicate how much you want the position. You have to establish an immediate emotional and mental connection in what is admittedly a stressful situation.

An actor, for instance, has to brave a cold room, read a

script that usually stinks, with a partner who also stinks, for a casting agent and execs who have already heard the material fifty times that day. But if she wants the job, she has to rise above the negativity, get into their guts, work from instinct, create the connection, heat up the room.

You do this not only by talking, but by listening. What does the guy who's hiring want to hear? Follow that lead; he or she will help you along, especially if there's a rapport. You'll both know it immediately. Instinctively.

Our new dog used the same technique to get us to take him home. We went to the adoption center and she watched as we checked out the possibilities. When we finally came to her cage she literally did whatever was in her power to make us know she wanted to be ours. She jumped into my lap; she licked me; she jumped up and down and rolled over four times. She couldn't actually say, "Boy, I'd love to live with you!" but believe me, that's what I heard.

On the ride home I thought of how, when I was twenty-four, I'd set my sights on a job in the William Morris Agency mailroom. "You're too old," the interviewer said.

"I'm not too old," I countered. "Plus, I'm willing to do anything I have to do to get the job. I really want to be here."

In other words, I had to make the guy understand that I wanted the job no matter what, without actually jumping into his lap, licking him, or rolling over.

By the time I got home that afternoon there was a message telling me to come to work the next Monday.

Then the real games began.

Know the Difference
Between Hot and Good

O NE HIT IS HOT. A career is good.

Hot can be the beginning of good, but in the end it's what you do with what you have. Longevity means staying in the game. How? Playing by the right rules. Manners. A little smarts. A lot of knowledge about what you do. A desire simply to do good work.

If you think you wrote the book on *anything*, you're wrong.

Unfortunately, the game these days is built on hot. Hot jocks. Hot actors. Hot agents. Hot trends. Hot shows. The cover of *Vanity Fair* is incestuously hot. That's great; heat sells. But six months later, who cares? Look at a top-ten list of the most powerful people in Hollywood from ten years ago. Make it five years ago. How many are around today? Quick, who was last year's hot supermodel?

There's nothing wrong with being hot as long as you have some perspective. Every day—hot or not—I wake up asking myself, "How can I stay myself?" Meaning, how can I not buy into my own heat, or at least not worry about whether or not I'm hot. How can I just do what I do, what I've always done, ignore the noise, and stay humble? Okay, not humble; how about not too full of myself?

That's part of the job description whether you're a star, a chef, a fireman, or a hooker.

Someone can be hot for many reasons, most of them having nothing to do with that person. She might be with a hot company. The whole industry may be hot. She might have landed in a hot film. Her team may be hot. One has to look at the big picture.

Take the writers on a hit sitcom. *Seinfeld* is a great example. The show couldn't have been hotter and the networks naturally wanted more of the same. So in their finite wisdom the powers that be at NBC, CBS, ABC, and FOX said, "Get some of those writers from *Seinfeld*."

When the season wound down they'd hire away a writer or writing team (who, if they'd been with the show a few seasons, now had *producer* titles), and say, "Look who we got!" They'd sign these writers for three years at two million dollars a year. And for what? The hope that they'd come up with some good ideas and create big hits.

Are the writers hot? It only seems that way. There were many writers on that show, but the bottom line is that Larry David and Jerry Seinfeld really came up with most everything, and the writers collaborated on the rest.

Three years later many of the hot writers with the big deals still haven't sold a script or had a pilot picked up, and when their contracts expired they couldn't get a job. With all that money, they can play a lot of golf.

Circumstances made them hot.

Look at the actors on *Seinfeld*. All are good actors who do quite well—and continue to. But the networks thought the *Seinfeld* magic would continue if each actor had his own show. What happened? Failed show. Failed show. Failed show. Meanwhile, only Larry David, who writes a show for himself on HBO, has a hit. I'm not knocking any of these people, but they were just on the right show, with the right chemistry, written by two geniuses, at the right time. Too bad they didn't have geniuses writing their next shows. And by the way, I'm not blaming them for doing those shows. I'd take the money and keep working, too. It's the networks expectations that were way off, and their overhyped belief that the public would automatically buy it. When big expectations crash, the sound of failure is louder. When will they learn?

Probably not soon enough.

The irony is that the more you worry about staying hot, the more likely you are to get cold. The trick is to keep doing exactly what you did before success arrived instead of trying to protect your accomplishments. Or copy them.

There's a big market for hot because, beyond the heat, the hope is that hot will become good. It happens, mostly to people with talent and a good attitude. How do you tell? Ask these questions: Do they think they're hot? Are they full of themselves? If so, chances are they're not paying attention to the work and they'll never get good.

My desires have always been straightforward: Do good

work and try to not get killed. I just want to continually expand my horizons and ignore the distractions.

But sometimes you need a little wake-up call. Mine was a classic.

Years ago, for a time, I couldn't have been hotter. I was so hot that maybe I had a little heat stroke. My wife and I got invited to the Golden Globes because someone I represented was nominated. We pulled up in the limo. Outside were hundreds of reporters and photographers. We got out of the car and stepped onto the red carpet. I straightened my tuxedo and looked up. Instead of flashbulbs popping and the press yelling my name, all I heard was one voice say, "Ah . . . it's no one."

I'm still around, though. I represent people who are good, not just hot. Longevity is the difference between the two, and learning how to tell the difference ensures it.

No One Is Ever Scared of a Fat Man

ACCEPT WHO YOU ARE, and use it to your advantage—
especially if it's a negative perception.

For instance, some people think that because I'm fat I must be jolly, maybe lazy. I understand. It's the stereotype.

In truth, when I was young I had lots of anger. I used to live in the husky department at Barneys. Too often I had to laugh my way into bed with a woman because—can you believe it?—some women don't find fat guys attractive. Today, I can't bend over to tie my shoes. I have to ask for a seat belt extension on airplanes. All my life, no one worried that I'd take their girlfriend. No one thought I looked better than them. No one thought I'd get their money. In most people's eyes, I was less than them—precisely because I was more.

To deal with it, I learned to make fun of my size myself. Once, I did a cameo part on Lily Tomlin's old TV show. It was a great sketch. The police were arresting all the fat people in Beverly Hills and I was one of them. But what can I do? My ass has always been wider than my shoulders. I was born with Russian peasant genes, not a thirty-two-inch waist. Well, I take that back; I probably was *born* with a thirty-two-inch waist.

The mistake is that because I'm fat, people believe I'm somehow vulnerable and easy to handle in a negotiation. Good. Let them underestimate me. Next thing you know I *do* steal the girlfriend, *do* out-negotiate, and *do* take the client. Turns out being heavyset has been wonderful for business. Sometimes I think good-looking guys have it a lot tougher than me.

We all have something we're not proud of, but I realized I had to learn to live with myself, and I decided I had no choice but to work real hard with what God gave me. Happily, that wasn't limited to extra heft. I was also funny, charming, and smart. The smarter you are the less you have to tell anyone you're smart, so I underplayed everything, was accepted as nonthreatening, and got into the game. I dressed casually—I think I was the first guy to go out in designer sweatsuits; I did it to be comfortable, not a trendsetter—and I've never played the part of mogul. As a result, people drop their guard around me and relax. Then I go to work. Ever try to negotiate with a fat guy? We can be mean: Marvin Davis, Harvey Weinstein, Hermann Goering. No one screws around with us for long. And when it's over, most of the time I manage to walk away with the lion's share without upsetting the other lions.

I know my reputation: I'm a little bit larger than life. For me, it's a great way to get ahead.

Who are you?

Tell 'Em Your Name
Even If They Already Know It

NOT LONG AGO I was at an after-hours business function when a guy about fifty, wearing a sharp suit and a big smile, strode briskly toward me with a look on his face that, even before he opened his mouth, screamed: "Bernie. What a surprise! Great to see you."

His hand was ready to grab mine for a hearty shake.

Unfortunately, I had a touch of what I call "damnesia" and couldn't remember his name.

What do you do when someone who clearly thinks he's your best friend is heading straight for you—and you don't have a clue who he is? How can you get out of a potentially embarrassing situation without ending up like Jackie Gleason's Ralph Kramden character nervously going, "huma-na, huma-na, huma-na?" Most people have no idea.

Here's what I do: Go on offense. Say, "Hi, I'm Bernie Brillstein."

They go, "Of course. You know *me*. Geez, I'm Joe Smith."

You go, "Yeah, I knew. I just didn't know if you knew who I was."

Turn it around and you're out of trouble.

Who's going to argue?

It's All Lies, and That's the Truth

YOU'VE HEARD THE OLD joke: "'Good morning,' he lied." That says it all.

People lie all the time. There are hundreds and thousands of lies. Lies of omission, of commission, big lies—and damn the consequences. Evil lies. I-don't-want-to-hurt-your-feelings lies. Let-me-get-the-fuck-outta-here lies. I-never-slept-with-that-woman lies. And to be fair, weapons-of-mass-destruction lies.

"I'll get back to you."

"Thanks for coming in."

"Let me run it past my group."

"Funny you called—I was just thinking about you."

"You killed 'em."

"I've never seen anything like it."

"The check's in the mail."

"You're the best."

"Unfortunately, we had an idea just like that."

And in sex:

"I never came like that in my life."

"I've never been with anyone like you."

"I'll call you tomorrow."

A common lie is "I can handle it." Now think of all the alcoholics and druggies. No one can *handle* it.

The biggest lie I ever heard—and there was absolutely *no reason* for it—was when I called a producer at ten o'clock in the morning, and his secretary said, "Sorry, he's out to lunch."

I said, "What? Did he have breakfast at four this morning?"

A big lie is when a director sleeps with an actress and says, "I'm going to give you the part," when he has no such intention. This happens more than you imagine—unless your imagination is as active as mine.

There's a big executive in Hollywood who is notorious for always saying, "Yes. I'll buy it." Then his business-affairs people unbuy it. If you call him on it he'll say, "Geez, I wanted to make a deal, but they couldn't." It's an old trick. He's the emperor. If he wanted the deal, they'd make it.

It's all bullshit and you know it's bullshit.

Lying always makes things worse. If you're involved with seven people and you tell one of them a lie, you then have to tell seven lies. The next time around, you triple it to cover up the other lies. I've never had that much time to waste, but people try to get away with lying because reality is not only perception, it's deception.

The people who *really* succeed are *not* liars.

You can usually tell when you hear the truth because it's delivered fast, and without elaboration. Recently, I had breakfast with a beautiful network executive. That morning I had taken a doctor-prescribed diuretic and I kept having to get up to pee. The third time she gave me an odd look. Was I making phone calls in the lobby? Was I on drugs? Was I having an affair with a waitress? Rather than make up some story I just told her the facts. She was a little embarrassed, but delighted.

The next time I had to get up and go to the bathroom we had a good laugh. And when we did business, she believed what I said.

Good Cop/Bad Cop
Means There's Two Bad Cops

WHEN YOU'RE TRYING TO make a deal, the other team may play good cop/bad cop. It's just what it sounds like: Someone opposite you at the negotiating table acts nicely, is sympathetic, understands your position. But his partner is willing to try and scare the hell out of you if you don't fall for the good cop's routine.

It's elementary psychological manipulation. You see it all the time on *Law & Order* when Detectives Briscoe and Green are trying to break a suspect. Sgt. Joe Friday and Officer Gannon did it, too. The routine even happens when you buy a car. Your salesman is the good guy; his boss, in the glass-walled office, is the bad guy. The salesman is supposedly "on your side," massaging the boss. Not true, of course. They're both bad cops, on the same side, doing their act to get you to part with your cash and take their car before the next shipment of cars comes in and they need room on the lot.

When you and your spouse want to buy a house, it's your

turn to play good cop/bad cop. You refrain from oohing and ahhing and saying anything positive while looking through the seller's closets and bedrooms because you know that if you want the place, they'll use your interest to hold firm the price or raise it.

When I was negotiating with Lord Lew Grade's company for Jim Henson and the Muppets to finally have their own TV show, I started by talking to Grade's American boss, Abe Mandel. Once we agreed we wanted to be in business his team talked to me and Jim's lawyer. Mandel was the good cop. When we had problems, Lord Grade—the nicest guy in the world—was the bad cop. Mandel would try to intimidate me by saying, "Lew won't like that."

When I didn't budge I eventually got the call from Lord Grade, who asked me what I was trying to do, saying I couldn't do it, and that the deal could fall through. I was respectful, but not afraid. I knew that Lord Grade wouldn't have called unless he really wanted Jim Henson. In fact, the calls signaled to me that my position had improved, even though Lord Grade wanted me to think the opposite. When the head of any company calls, it is usually to exert his influence to get you to accept a deal. He doesn't want to be embarrassed by not getting something. Believe me, if he didn't care and you had already blown the deal, he wouldn't call.

So I said no to him, and by the way, it wasn't out of greed but because I thought I was right. I believed in my position. I also believed that when the bad cop takes the time to call and maybe even threaten you, it means you might get what you want. His side is probably nervous. No bad cop calls to give good news.

So don't buy the bluster. Each negotiation has a guy with more to gain and a guy with more to lose. And there's always a guy who steps in with a hammer, and when he does you can usually get what you want. Stand your ground, with decency—not arrogance—and eventually the good cop will be on the line, calling to say, "You got the deal."

I got the Muppet deal and we were on the air for five years.

Sublimate Your Ego for Cash—
And Other Ways to Get What You Want

I F YOU MEET A beautiful woman and desire her, and you know that she loves Las Vegas (and you hate it), all things being equal, if you'd like to sleep with her, you improve your chances by taking her to Vegas. If you're a she and he's a he, it works both ways, by the way.

Simple.

You sublimate what you want to give her what she wants so that you get what you want.

I call that the "You Attitude."

I've been this way naturally, all my life—sensitive to the other person's needs so that I can also get what I want—but I didn't know what it was called until Professor DeFillipi wrote it on the blackboard the first day of a business management course I took at NYU.

Believe it or not, as obvious as this bit of common sense seems, lots of people *don't* think of the other guy.

They should. The "You Attitude" is at the heart of what it

;ood manager, at the heart of getting a job, at the
ng. Don't worry about what you want to sell,
what the customer wants to buy. What does he
need? Get into his head. Listen instead of talk, and when you
do talk you don't say what *you* want to say, say what the other
guy wants to hear. Follow his lead; he will help you along.

I call it sublimating my ego for cash.

There are good salesmen and bad. You can walk into a
store, ask about a product, and the guy behind the counter will
sometimes point and say, "It's in that section over there." The
guy who wants to *sell* the product will say, "Come with me. I'll
take you." Even if you're indecisive about buying, more often
than not you probably will because of the extra effort—especially
if it's clear that the salesman listened to what you wanted and
gave it to you.

Thinking of the other guy is not the same as being a wuss;
it just saves you a lot of aggravation in life. And if the other
guy is the right kind of guy he'll know when something is
important to you. The "You Attitude" is not a one-way street.

I practiced the "You Attitude" even when I was red-hot
because I never forgot that I was also Bernie Brillstein, just
lucky to be there.

Here's how I once used the "You Attitude": When I managed John Belushi, he did *Animal House* for $35,000. No one
knew it would be a hit, but it ended up being thought of as a
new kind of comedy for a new generation. Afterward, Universal Pictures wanted him badly. We wanted more money and a
three-picture deal. As luck would have it, Universal had never
taken an option on John's services.

I knew the guy I was negotiating with at Universal would be at least fair because they couldn't *afford* to lose Belushi at the time. And I wanted to give him what he wanted as long we got what we wanted. But instead of naming a price—I didn't really know what to ask for anyway—I used the "You Attitude" and said, "Give me the price *you* want to pay." I also said, "You have one shot," which immediately raised his price 25 percent. "If I like it, he's yours." Plus—and the only thing this has to do with attitude is that I must have had a lot of balls even to suggest it—I had Universal send me $250,000 just to listen and I promised not to make a deal with another studio until they made a proposal.

They came up with really good numbers: $1 million, $1.85 million, and $2.5 million, for the three pictures.

We made the deal.

Guys who try to screw you in business just because they think they can, practice the "Me Attitude." But they're really only screwing themselves and their clients because one day they will be cold and no one will care what they want.

If you treat people fairly, think about their needs as well as your own, you will always be ahead. By the way, there's nothing wrong with a little "I Attitude" at times. I tell every client, "Give them two and you take one, and it will keep you in the business forever."

If You Want to Make a Great Deal
You Have to Be Willing to Blow a Great Deal

No MATTER WHAT YOU read in the papers, negotiating is probably the least dramatic thing I do. Most of the talk about "the art of the deal" is after-the-fact self-aggrandizement. Sometimes I think that if we lived the lives we read about, we couldn't call them lives at all.

Making deals is about finding the proper strategy, not about whose dick is bigger. When people want to be in business together, forget the financials, the paperwork, the redline copy, and all the minutiae. The basics—the desire to work together, the agreement to make the deal—are done in two days, often less.

However, occasionally the proceedings get dirty and mean, and deals get hung up in the paperwork because of emotions, greed, or both. Then it begins to drag on and on. You get crazy. Confused. Temporarily manic-depressive. Eventually, the only way to reach a conclusion that you think is fair, and in which you believe that no one gets the better of everything, is be willing to let it fall apart. Believe me, if it doesn't r principles today, then the aggravation you're expe-...encing now will only become greater later on.

You've got to mean it, though, and be willing to lose the sale.

I promise that's when you'll find out how much the other guy really wants to be in business. It always comes down to you. They have to know to respect you when you say, "Take it or leave it." And when you do, don't give too much information. Cut the flowery bullshit when you're bottom-lining, and be like the police: "Surrender or we're coming in." Even if the other side really wants to make the deal, that doesn't mean they won't try to nickel-and-dime you. Stick to your guns. Try setting a deadline. The hat salesman says, "My lowest price for a gross is twelve dollars." The buyer, who's been hondling for seven weeks (and thinks he won't lose the deal because he's still in the game and you're trying to be nice), says, "But I can only pay eleven dollars." If twelve dollars is your number, then at some point you have to draw the line. "Look. I have the hats. I'm willing to ship them for my price. If you don't tell me by six o'clock, it's over."

I'd much rather get a take-it-or-leave-it offer from anyone than do the negotiation dance. Give me the facts and let me say yes or no quickly. If you come up with my price, right or wrong, I'm there. Otherwise it's a waste of time.

The trouble with the business world today is that no one says, "Kiss my ass" (or worse). Sports. Show business. Media. Manufacturing. Whatever. Everyone is afraid to lose. Everyone squeezes for the extra dollar. Everyone says, "Oh, I *need* it."

Later, they brag, "You know how much I got it for?"

I never do that because I never got any client money that someone didn't *want* to pay. If you think you're such a good negotiator, just try and get a wad of cash for an unknown, or for a bad idea. It's all about the buyer's need. If they think you're hot, if a product is desirable, if someone wants what you have, they pay.

Hitler could sell a sitcom if a network wanted it enough.

This behavior is in part due to the pressure to be "Number One." Or the pressure to not let your opponents get it. In a business dominated by short-term thinking, it's tough to see money—or simply victory—slip away. The fear that your client will be pissed is chilling. But it's the best way. If you're moral and honest, don't just use your "principles" as a negotiating ploy, otherwise you'll be known for using tactics cheaply. Stick to your code and people will gossip about that as much as anything else, and your reputation will precede you—not exceed you.

Who wants to win and then discover that the prize wasn't worth the aggravation?

My advice: Be a grown-up. Let it go. Don't spend all your time trying to get the other guy to be a grown-up, too. You can't run anyone else's life. It's bad enough riding the roller coaster of your own needs and emotions, why ride someone else's? You can't train the other guy. He'll go to lawyer after lawyer until he finds someone who tells him he's right. Then there will be another six months of negotiations. You can't teach someone common sense.

By the way, it helps to play the negotiating game with

people who understand how it's played. That can be fun. Energizing. Mostly, people are clueless.

Too many people fail at negotiation because they're frightened they might ask for too much, or too little, or break something. All I can say is, "Get over it." I used to gamble a lot and if you bust big at a craps table—not a penny left, no credit, no friends to call—your mind flips faster than when you have to figure the angles on some Hollywood contract. If you're unlucky and have to leave town with only a complimentary pack of cigarettes and the change from the five bucks someone loaned you for a cab, and all you think about on the trip home is, "Oh, God. Where will I get the money? How can I keep them from breaking my legs?" business deals don't seem that life or death.

When I was twenty-eight I owed a Vegas casino $70,000. My fantasy was not a hot night with a woman in a garter belt, or a booking for big dough. It was going to Yankee Stadium on a Sunday, to a double-header with 72,000 people, and having everyone give me a dollar to get me out of my hole. I only made $12,000 a year, most of which went to rent and alimony. *That's* cause for anxiety. But I made it through and that's why today I can enter the negotiating arena with a unique frame of mind.

In plain English: I'm not scared.

Nothing is more valuable.

Once, Brad Grey, who now runs Brillstein-Grey, and I were negotiating a deal for our client, the actor Ed O'Neill. Every time we said something the guy at the other end of the table worked out the figures on his calculator. After three times I got pissed off. When he excused himself for a minute, I took the calculator and left the building. Ed O'Neill now has the calculator on his mantel—and by the way, he got every penny we wanted.

If someone goes back on a deal point, I just leave the table. "Bye, gentlemen. The meeting's over."

When I walk out I don't yell. In fact, I usually don't say anything. Most of the time they run after me. I've had network presidents chase me through parking lots. As long as your clients trust you and know you're acting in their best interests—and you'd better be—you're in the clear. If the deal dies, it was probably meant to. So you blew the commission. Trust me, you'll get it all back and maybe more some other time, when the deal is right.

If you lose, you lose. Another deal will come along. For goodness' sake, bet on yourself. You're great at what you do. People need you. No one else is as passionate. But if the minute you wake up in the morning a random thought about the deal gives you a stomachache, get rid of it.

And then, guess what: Six months later—and sometimes immediately—you'll hear, "Are you still interested?" It's happened to me a million times. I love hearing people say, "Boy, I wish I'd made that deal with you." It's great. Well, it's not really great, but it's great.

How do you negotiate to buy a house? There's the asking price, there's the selling price, there's the real price. You always go in with your spouse. First you say, "No more than . . . ," then you see the house. Then it's a different ball game. Then you're talking to one another and you see the look on his or her face. All of a sudden it's another ten grand. The seller knows that all this is going on. Eventually the two of you have to sit down and go, "Look, we're not going to go a penny more than X, and we're sticking to it." And you have to be willing to lose the house.

Your bottom line is never as good as saying, "I am telling you, it's over at six o'clock."

And don't give too much time or leeway.

Finally, there's a life span to a deal. If no one's called you back for three or four days and said, "We're in the ballpark," there'd better be a very good reason, or it's not a deal. When they want you, you can't stop them from coming after you. You can tell by the first phone call what's going on. If the other guy says, "I'm coming over now and I'm not leaving until I have the deal," you're in great shape. If he says, "What's the soonest you can meet?" you're in good shape. If he says, "Oh, I'm very glad to see your client is available and interested. I'll get back to you," then ninety-nine times out of a hundred it's never going to happen. You're just being strung along, forced to live on hope, afraid that if you get impatient you'll blow the whole thing. Hope's a nice thing, but not if someone's jerking you around.

Forget it. It's already over.

Always Have a Backup Plan

YEARS AGO MIKE OVITZ, former head of Hollywood's Creative Artists Agency (CAA), and from 1985–1995 the media- and self-professed "most powerful man in show business," asked me to see a puppeteer client named Paul Fusco. I already had the world's best in Jim Henson, but I figured what the hell. Fusco walked into my office carrying a large black plastic garbage bag. I was immediately curious and probably a little nervous; who knew what was in the crumpled sack? I found out when Fusco pulled out this weird-looking furry brown creature. It looked like a bear with a long pig's snout. His name was ALF (short for Alien Life Form). Fusco explained that ALF came from the planet Melmac, then insulted me in ALF's gravelly, burlesque voice. It was hysterical.

I called the writer Tom Patchett. He and Fusco worked up a pitch for the series. I called Brandon Tartikoff at NBC and set up a meeting.

We arrived early, like I always do, to check out the attitudes and the environment.

A secretary showed Fusco, Patchett, and our CAA agent into a conference room, where Tartikoff and a couple other executives waited. I sat Fusco next to Tartikoff. I was at Fusco's left. We made the usual small talk designed to lull and disarm everyone into instant receptivity and nonresistence. Then Patchett started to pitch the show.

Unfortunately, Patchett got lost in a long-winded explanation of the puppet and the backstory and right away I knew we were going into the toilet. It looked to me as if everyone had tuned out, save for Tartikoff, and he was close. But Fusco and I had a contingency plan. I kicked him under the table. He took ALF out of his garbage bag, put it on his hand, did the voice, sneezed, wiped his nose, and then smeared it on Tartikoff's sleeve.

"I get it," said Tartikoff, laughing. "Let's go!" Boom. Deal. We walked out with a pilot order.

The first step to a backup plan is asking a simple question: "What if?"

Believe it or not, some people never ask. Take the movie *Gigli,* with Ben Affleck and J.Lo. Everyone took it for granted it would be a big hit. No one *ever* thought it would die like it did. After all, it had two big stars. You couldn't turn around without seeing the hype. Someone once said there's no such thing as too much publicity—or bad publicity. Yeah? Bullshit. All of a sudden America turned off. Did they sense the movie was just thrown together for the money? Was it just a bad picture? Who knows. But I'll bet that in the many, many meetings to plan the picture's release and marketing campaign no one ever said, "Hey Irving. What if it doesn't work? What do we do next week?"

If you think ahead, you can figure alternative ways to get what you want when you encounter stumbling blocks.

For instance, I can't buy suits off the rack. I'm too big. I never thought about it much until my luggage didn't arrive on a trip to Rome. You can't just waltz into a Big & Tall store around the corner from the Coliseum. Luckily my wife, Carrie, found a tailor who made me two suits. Cost me thousands. Now I check ahead for someplace to buy clothes in my size whenever I go out of town. You never know when the airlines will lose your bags—and neither do they.

I also check alternate flights and always have a list handy.

Sometimes my assistant has to call a packed restaurant for a dinner reservation in an hour. The restaurant says okay, but I believe in Murphy's Law. What if when I get there the maitre d' I know isn't working? I have the name of everyone who ever confirmed and reconfirmed the reservation. Sometimes a twenty-dollar bill is part of the backup plan; I'm that paranoid. But I've never been turned away.

If You Can't Whip It Out,
Don't Play the Game

YOU'RE IN A FRIENDLY poker game. No one puts in money up front. You say you'll take $200 in chips and everyone will settle up at the end.

You'd better.

If you lose and don't have the money to cover your debt, you've played under false pretenses. In gambling we call keeping your word being able to "whip it out," as in whipping out the money. In the old days, in Vegas, not being able to whip it out could result in some thuggery and a hospital stay. Today the only thing that will get killed is your reputation.

Life runs on honor.

If you tell someone you'll take care of a situation immediately, you do it. If you find you can't, say so quickly.

Doing the honorable thing doesn't always guarantee success, but you gotta do it anyway. Take the 2003 World Series. The Red Sox's manager decided, "I'm going with my best pitcher in the seventh game. And I'm not going to take him out when the game's on the line." Any schmuck in the world could have put in a relief pitcher. He didn't. The manager guessed wrong, and he was fired. But he was honorable.

Dishonor takes many forms. Some people will scoot to the bathroom when a meal is done and come back asking, "Did the check come yet?"

If you buy a custom-made present and say, "I must have this by December 18," and the guy says he'll have it, he'd better be able to "whip out" the gift at the appointed hour. If he took the order just to take the order, time to go to a different store. The only excuse I'll accept is a reasonably early warning call explaining that there's going to be a delay. If he's nice I probably won't be so quick to tell the guy to stick it.

By the way, we always know intuitively which people are scamming us, even if we don't want to admit it. Anyone who has kids understands. There are no bigger con artists than children. If you tell me you're going to do something and don't, you'll lose not my love, but my respect.

Here's how bad—and ridiculous—it can get. I once lent someone $5,000 and he paid me back $3,000. He didn't say the other $2,000 would come soon. He didn't even acknowledge the outstanding balance. Why? Because he made believe he only borrowed $3,000. I don't get it? Did he think maybe the $2,000 didn't mean anything to me just because I could live without it? He missed the point: What meant a lot to me was his character—which apparently stunk. I marked him "dead" and went on with my life; I didn't even remind him.

If your boss offers you a $50,000 bonus and then gives you

only $35,000, it's clearly not a place you should stick around for a long time.

I always give people enough rope to hang themselves. The truth is that I love to catch people being dishonorable. Maybe it's because I have such tough rules for myself. Maybe it makes me feel better about myself. If someone thinks that makes me a schmuck, fine. It's a cheap price to pay for never having to deal with some people again.

If you want to play the game, play honorably. You can only stiff me once.

Success Begins with Being Yourself

WHETHER YOU'RE NEW ON the job or a veteran, the pressure to conform to the culture of the workplace is enormous. Every business has its own psyche, and they hire people whom they believe will fit that mind-set. IBM people dress one way. Apple Computer people another. George Steinbrenner buys baseball players he believes fit into the Yankee mold—dignified, above it all, carrying themselves as if they were champions. (Steinbrenner is not anything like that himself; he just hires guys who personify the image of what he'd like to be.) You can line up employees from every talent agency in Hollywood and tell just by the way they look for whom they work.

Everyone wants to fit in, catch the boss's eye, maybe take the fast track to a vice presidency.

Okay. If you want to be a Babbitt, be a Babbitt. (Note: Read Sinclair Lewis.) Act like everyone else, be afraid like everyone else, keep your ideas to yourself like everyone else, do your job and try to stay under the radar like everyone else.

It's a guaranteed path directly to the middle of the pack.

Some people want that, and God bless them; but the real successes don't conform.

I'm not saying break the dress code and show butt-crack; but find some way to stand out. Any way. The best method is to work with who you are. Don't go looking for a style, find it in yourself. If all talent agents wear fashionable Armani and you wear Armani, you're not in style. You're in what other people think is style.

Style, of course, is not only the way you dress, but the way you act. You owe it to yourself to be yourself and see if other people can stand it. I'm not saying be arrogant; moderation is fine. But if you have a sense of humor, please show it. If you have a great brain, show it. If you have a great beauty, show it.

I certainly have my own style. I'm a loud laugher, an out-size player; people know when I walk into the room. I'm never going to be suave. I have a Falstaffian manner. People say I'm larger than life. Fine with me.

But at William Morris in the fifties and sixties, I wore an alpaca sweater instead of the required suit. I wasn't trying to break the rules; I was big. I felt better in a sweater than in a jacket. My work improved. If someone didn't understand it, that was their problem. You couldn't fault my output.

If you don't have an extra fifty pounds to work with, try showcasing what you're best at. Do you know more about baseball than anyone else? Have you read every Shakespeare play? Are you a hit with the ladies or gentlemen?

Do whatever works (appropriately) to get people to talk

about you because, if they do, that means you're different—
and that's good news, not bad news. Forget the conventional
wisdom that if you stick out you'll attract trouble. If *that* happens, you can leave and start your own company. In fact, if
you're different enough, you'll probably want to.

Honestly, this works, on any level. Let yourself hang out.
If you go to a restaurant regularly, isn't there always a waiter
whose area you'd rather sit in? He never says anything personal
to you except maybe, "Good evening, Mr. Smith," but there's
something about his demeanor that makes you happier; therefore his tips will be bigger and he'll have more regular cus-
tomers. Soon he'll open his own restaurant.

Find a job where you can express yourself.

Every year I talk to the mailroom kids and interns at my
company. One year this kid raised his hand and asked a question that took a lot of nerve—even if he'd been around five
years. It may not mean a lot outside show business but he
wanted to know if there was a conflict of interest between our
management company managing actors, and our production
company producing their TV shows. There isn't, for reasons
too complicated to go into now. All I can say is that we can't
force any client to let us produce their shows, and we can't
force any client to act in shows that we produce. Anyway, the
question was bold and could have been taken as impertinent—
or wrong. But I understood that he was not only thinking
ahead of the pack, but had the guts to voice an opinion. I never
forgot that kid, and he's since become a success in the business.
He let himself hang out. He took a chance, a calculated risk,

that I wouldn't say, "Go to hell, it's none of your business." He made a difference. You always take note. As a boss I'd rather deal with someone real than with a cookie-cutter personality.

There is a flip side, of course. You have to know when to conform. Certain situations demand a suit. Other times you just have to shut up. There is a game we all have to play, but we can still play it creatively. Those who try to be creative usually get away with more because *people expect it of creative people and tolerate it.*

One of my favorite sayings is: "They haven't caught me yet."

It Never Gets Better Than the First Date

YOU SEE A WOMAN. You think she's beautiful. You ask her out. You both show up showered, well-dressed, a little nervous, hoping for approval. You're both auditioning—and you're dying to get that part over with so you can figure out if it's going any further. Can you accept each other's look, dress, personality, desires, dreams? If you do, if you smell potential, you go out again, put on the full-court press. Suddenly your time together is better than you ever thought things could be. Maybe you even consummate the relationship. In bed, your manners are perfect. In the afterglow you think, "Wow. I really made it. Here I am. It's wonderful."

Then you see hairs on her nipples. Or you fart.

Unfortunately, it never gets better than the first date—metaphorically; sometimes literally. The mistake people make is they think "The Moment" is forever.

Courtship and seduction always feel great, but expecting the feeling to last forever, whatever the situation, is crazy.

that and you'll be able to move past the honey-
the good beginning on tap, and focus on real life.
same in business.

the initial meeting you were both considerate,
charming, persuasive, attentive. You met again and although
there were some rough spots in the negotiations, you both
worked hard to get to the final handshake. But the minute the
deal is done, the doubt takes hold. Now everyone wonders
whether it was—or will be—worth it.

Here's the good news and the bad news. The good news:
You've got a new business deal. The bad news: You've got a
new business deal. It's great to sign on the dotted line, but now
you have to do the work. Do it well and new deals will invariably result.

Winners Make the Tough Calls

IT'S EASY TO CALL someone when they've just had a hit, but it's more important to make the call when someone is cold, when they've flopped, when there's nothing to say. You get a sinking feeling in the stomach, you don't want to pick up the phone, but you've got to. Leaders and winners make the tough calls. And whomever's on the other end of the line never forgets. Truth is, they're waiting at home hoping to hear from you, from anyone.

Bill Maher floundered for three or four years before *Politically Incorrect* hit it big, yet I spoke to him every week. After I said, "How are you?" I mostly listened. Then I said, "Hey, Bill, what you do is different. You don't look like everyone else, you don't sound like everyone else. It takes longer for guys like you to make it, but when you do it's really going to be there." And then it was. He's never forgotten that I cared.

People appreciate it when you leave out the bullshit. Yet most of the time—using my business as an example—an actor's agent will say, "Don't worry, I'll take care of it. There's another job around the corner." The manager will say, "We're working on this." The lawyer will say, "Oh, don't worry, we're fine." All garbage. Someone has to say, "We're screwed. We better start at the beginning." I've seen people literally disappear from my business because everyone's telling them it's all okay—instead of the truth.

I had a client whose TV show had been on four years, the hit ratings took a dive and were terrible, and my instinct told me that it was about to be canceled. I called him immediately and said, "I don't know for sure, but I think it's over." After I hung up I imagined myself in his head and thought he must feel terrible getting such bad news without any window dressing. I called back and said, "I just want to explain . . ."

He said, "Bernie, you don't have to. I love you because you always tell me the truth. Everyone else is telling me don't worry. But I am worried, and rightfully so. Thank you for calling, I really appreciate it."

My reputation is based on being as straight a shooter as I can humanly be and get by. It's not a moral standard, it's an identity. As I suspected, the show was canceled and all my client was left with was knowing who he could trust.

It's true that no one wants to get bad news. Imagine if your best friend took you aside and said, "You know, your wife's been cheating on you." But he tells you *because* he knows you're going to find out one way or another—and he's your best friend. Chances are he'll stay your best friend.

Have an Opinion Even If It's Wrong

You're in a club and see six beautiful women at the bar. You can't talk to them all, so you choose one. You follow your instinct on what you think is the right move for you. You could meet the woman of your dreams. You could also have the worst night of your life—but the same could be true had you gone with any of the other five. At least you chose.

Bottom line: You went with your gut and took your shot.

No one likes a guy without an opinion. At worst you could be wrong. I'm not saying you walk in the first day and tell everyone what you think. You listen. You survey. You pay attention to what people who've been there longer say. There's a difference between someone with an opinion and a loudmouth. The loudmouth will say stupid things and kill himself.

I form opinions quickly. I don't have the patience to mull over everything. People who ponder perpetually are putzes. You can examine every side of a problem and still not have the answer because most everything in life is a guess—and in business it's even worse. It's all based on guts. You know you *could* be wrong, but if you live by the credo "I may be wrong," then you're mostly *going* to be wrong. If you don't believe in yourself you're not going to make it. You might even have great instincts, but you'll ignore them and be a loser because you're afraid of what *may* happen.

Then nothing happens.

Follow the Loser

THERE ARE MANY WAYS to climb the ladder at work.

At William Morris I could have gotten out of the mailroom the traditional way by impressing an agent into hiring me as his assistant. But I was in a hurry, so when the company's head of publicity asked me if I wanted to work for him, I jumped at the chance. My friends thought I'd made a mistake. "Publicity is grunt work," they said. "You'll go nowhere. Don't take the job."

They were partly right: My new boss, Jerry, had been doing the job for years and had hit a dead end. Whatever ambition he'd once had—maybe—was long gone. His personality was unremarkable, his performance ho-hum at best. But I'd thought of something they hadn't. The publicity office was opposite a big agent's office, and when you're trying to move up—*if* you're trying to move up—proximity to power is priceless. Also, writing bios for our clients and making up publicity packages with their head shots would give me

exposure to almost every agent and client in the
And finally, my instinct told me that Jerry was a
who might not last much longer. Since we were a
two   son department, I imagined him getting fired and me
getting his job.

Most people won't admit that, but there's not an ambitious person in the world who at some point doesn't think they can do the job as well or better than their boss. Even a supermarket box boy looks at the manager and thinks, "Hey, *this* guy's an idiot. I can run this store." And believe me, no smart boss doesn't know that the new kid might one day be calling the shots.

Pretty soon I was. Did my takeover fantasies have anything to do with Jerry being let go? No. There's no voodoo here. Nor did I do anything untoward to sabotage or undercut him. I just had an instinct that he would soon be gone. But I wasn't so arrogant to assume that just following the loser was all it took to move up. It's a two-part package. I made sure to work my ass off and ingratiate myself with the higher-ups so that when Jerry got canned I was the natural replacement. You should always do the second part no matter what, but the climb can be a bit easier if you pick your spot.

I got my next job in the commercials department at William Morris the same way. I thought my boss looked unhappy. I thought I had better ideas than he did for how to grow the business. I did my job, smiled, acted nonthreatening, and waited for him to fall apart. When he did I took over.

God Helps Himself; You've Got to Ask

I N 1969 I WAS getting a $40,000-a-year royalty for *Hee Haw*. The show was originally my idea, but the producers I hired did the heavy lifting and made a lot more money. I didn't mind—for a while. Then I got pissed off and thought that because it was such a huge hit and there was so much money coming in that I ought to get more. Even my ex-wife nagged me, "They're killing you, Bernie." But I was afraid that if I asked for more they'd get mad and fire me. (Even though the show was my idea, I couldn't take it with me.) Finally, I found the balls to speak up. I went to the executive producer and said, "I'm not getting enough money."

"Well, how much do you want?" he asked.

I said, "I want . . . $75,000." A fortune at the time.

"You got it," he said, without missing a beat.

"Whoa. What do you mean, I have it?"

"Just that," he said, "you have it."

Was it my balls that got me the money? Only partly.

"If I got it so easily, why didn't you just give it to me?"

He said, "Why didn't you ask?"

I should have known better because something similar had happened to a friend of mine who'd graduated from NYU as a young accountant. He was really smart. He knew a guy who owned a grocery chain and he had a problem his accountant wasn't solving. He asked my friend to solve the problem, which he did. Then he asked how much he owed him and my friend said, "Nothing. I did it for you." Two months later the owner hired another accountant—not my friend. He asked what happened. "Didn't I help you?"

The answer: "If you don't believe in yourself, I don't believe in you."

Sometimes believing in yourself means asking for the money.

Always Smell the Room

I BASE EVERYTHING ON my gut. It doesn't matter if it's in business or life. You've got to train yourself to feel what's going on, what's in the air. If you're willing to smell the room, you'll know exactly what to do. If you're willing to be oblivious, then you're in trouble.

When you go to a meeting, get there early. Look at the people's faces. Try and get the rhythm of the place so you don't feel like a stranger in the environment. If the appointment's at 1:30, don't walk in at 1:29. I like to sit in the lobby for a bit and absorb the atmosphere in the same way that I walk around the crap tables in Vegas, checking out the action before throwing the dice. I'm probing. Testing. Acclimating. I'm like a boxer warming up, a batter swinging in the on-deck circle, or someone shooting hoops before the game. This isn't ooga-booga. I'm looking at secretaries' mannerisms; I'm gauging the ebb and flow. I want to find out if the environment is hostile or friendly.

Some days it's not right to pitch an idea, do business, or

try for a job. If you were waiting to meet me and I made you sit in the lobby for thirty or forty-five minutes, you should know instinctively that the timing for whatever you want is wrong. Sure, I want to hear what you have to say—after all, I took the meeting—but I'm also so far behind I probably won't be concentrating.

(And by the way, if anyone makes you wait for a half an hour without an assistant coming out to apologize, you should have walked out fifteen minutes earlier. I would.)

When you get to my office, it takes a very big guy to say, "Okay, let's forget today. I know you're harried. Let's just talk for a few minutes and we'll do it another time."

I might still say, "Don't worry, just go ahead and pitch," but it also takes a big man on my end to appreciate your instinct—and reschedule.

These days, on my side of the desk, I also have to smell the room before a meeting. I do it automatically. When a potential new client comes to see me, I can usually tell, as he walks through the door with his agent and lawyer and entourage, how things will go just through body language.

There are always little tip-offs.

For instance, one afternoon the late Frank Wells, a very bright, imposing guy who was for a time Michael Eisner's number two guy at Disney, dropped by my office to settle up with me on a deal we'd made for Lorne Michaels to produce pictures at Warner Bros. We'd taken the deal instead of another one offered by Barry Diller, then at Paramount Pictures. The Warner guys, including Wells, had made a big fuss over Lorne, liberally tossing around words like "career."

Unfortunately, after the first picture it didn't work out. We went to Paramount.

Eventually it was time to settle up and Wells came to my office. I was nervous and thought I'd have a fight on my hands to get Lorne what they owed him. The Warner guys were notoriously tough. When Wells arrived, my brother-in-law, who worked with me, buzzed me on the intercom to let me know. Then, perhaps as just an offhand comment, he said Wells was really perspiring. Something in my head clicked: It wasn't *that* hot outside. That's when I knew Wells was nervous, too, and I could use that to be home free. I got all the money they owed us.

Never Trust a Man Who Walks You to the Elevator with His Arm Around Your Shoulder

Years ago, when I ran Lorimar's movie studio and Warner Communications (now Time Warner) was about to buy it, I flew to New York to meet with the late Steve Ross, who ran the company. I wanted to save my job.

Ross, who started out working for his father-in-law's Manhattan funeral parlor and rose to run one of the world's then-biggest media companies, was a handsome, impressive guy. His management style was to let his trusted lieutenants run their fiefdoms with virtual autonomy—he backed up their decisions—which in turn created incredible loyalty to him. Ross also believed in rewarding his top employees, and let them use the company's vacation homes and corporate jets. Talk about perks.

And yet, I knew that however imperious Ross seemed to the business community, he was originally a kid from Flatbush, in Brooklyn. Like me, he was streetwise and could talk with people on all levels. That's why when I went to see him about staying in charge of Lorimar Pictures. I thought I had a fighting chance.

We talked for a while and he gave me the impression that when he took over nothing would change. What I heard—what I wanted to hear—was that I had nothing to worry about. When we were done, he put his arm around my shoulder and walked me to the elevator, sweet-talking the whole way.

A week later, a press release reflected our conversation. A couple weeks later I flew to New York to cast my vote for the merger.

When I got back to Los Angeles, I realized I'd swallowed Ross's bait hook, line, and sinker. My new marching orders were on my desk. Sure, I still ran Lorimar, but any power I'd had before visiting Ross had been gutted. I couldn't spend more than one hundred grand on any project without the approval of my new bosses, Bob Daly and Terry Semel.

I couldn't figure out what had happened. I thought maybe it was payback for green-lighting *Dangerous Liaisons* the morning before voting for the merger. I'd done it because I had an odd feeling in my gut, and didn't want to take any chances it wouldn't get made. But pretty soon I realized that Ross didn't even think on that level. He just wanted to close the deal and he told me whatever he thought I needed to hear to get my vote.

I learned a costly lesson.

Beware of people who are too nice, or who immediately play the card they think will get them close to you. Beware the too quickly established intimacy. Beware of anyone who knows too much about you. Everyone needs a bullshit detector.

For instance, because I'm Jewish, I'm always leery of anyone who immediately speaks Yiddish to me in a business context. (Whatever your cultural background, substitute appropriately.) For instance, once, when I was still at Lorimar, my secretary said, "Simon Wiesenthal is calling."

Simon Wiesenthal is the world's most famous Nazi-hunter.

"That's one of my idiot friends making a joke," I said dismissively.

"Well, how would I know?" she said.

I picked up the phone. "Hello?"

The voice on the other end started in with the Yiddish, telling me he's heard of me, and what a wonderful person I am. (All true, of course). Immediately, I realized it actually *was* Wiesenthal. Now, I was impressed, and I said so. But part of me wondered, Why is he calling *me?* He must really want something, and I'm not talking about a charitable donation.

After wishing me a happy Passover, Wiesenthal said, "By the way, why won't Richard Dreyfuss play my life in a miniseries?"

I was right. The Brillstein Company, which was also part of Lorimar, managed Dreyfuss. Wiesenthal had an angle all along.

Fortunately, I had learned this lesson early in my career, at the William Morris Agency. When I moved from the commercials department to television, a beautiful model who'd done a famous cigar commercial called me. I'd represented her in commercials, and now that I'd been promoted, she wanted to take me to lunch. I agreed—hey, she was gorgeous—and we went to Alfredo's.

Over the fettuccine she kept saying, "I'm so proud of you" and other complimentary things. She was so major league–

looking, with her yellow dress and her blonde hair spilling everywhere, that it was all I could do to keep from spilling my lunch on myself. When she got the check she said, "Do you have to go right back to work?"

"No," I said, "I don't *have* to go back."

We went to her apartment. I thought I was sophisticated, but I was not sophisticated. We got inside, got undressed, and the next thing I know we got down to business and, at the time, it was probably the best business I'd ever done.

Afterward, she popped out of bed, rummaged around in a closet for her portfolio, and spread a bunch of 11-by-14 pictures on the floor.

"Which are the nicest, Bernie?" she asked.

It was like a cold shower. I looked at the pictures, said, "That and that." Then I said, "Good-bye." Never saw her again, but that's when I began to understand how this aspect of the game really worked.

There's No Such Thing As a Good Divorce

N O ONE GETS DIVORCED because they get along. Even though you started out as great friends, the sex was hotter than a triple-X movie, and you promised to raise the children together, marriages break up. It's the same in business. Whether you're a dress salesman who has suddenly lost a steady client, or you and your writing partner created the hottest show on TV, made millions from the deal, and it looked like the future was wide open, things happen. Despite the thrilling start and the giddy high, somehow the relationship has turned into an irritant and you can't stand each other. Suddenly years have passed that you can't reclaim. It doesn't matter how much money and fame came your way, if you could have reached each other on any level the relationship wouldn't have ended.

One or both of you are pissed off.

It's over.

So why do the parties, especially in business, pretend it's an amiable separation when nine times out of ten it's ugly and bitter? Why not just admit the truth and move on?

I know: It's classier that way. You think, How nice, when you read about it. But it usually isn't true and it leads to a big surprise and extra emotional baggage when it happens to you. And you thought it would be easy, right?

Divorce isn't a simple decision for anyone. I take it hard when a client leaves me. That doesn't happen often, but it happens. A few years ago I helped Richard Dreyfuss to his feet by getting him a decent fee to make *Down and Out in Beverly Hills,* which led to a string of more lucrative pictures. Then he was gone. He probably had his own reason for leaving, but he still hasn't told me. I take nothing away from his talent; we spent so much time together it seemed like we were actually friends. My mistake. We may not have made the details of our divorce public, but it was painful and we've never been friends again.

Even if I leave first, I feel miserable. I still feel like I did something wrong. Then, when they hook up with someone else, I feel worse.

When a potential U.S. president interviews six vice presidential candidates and can choose only one, do you think the other five stay close friends?

When a baseball team manager fires a player, do you think they keep hanging out together?

So why does anyone believe the press release that divorcing parties bear no enmity and wish each other well? When it's me, I don't wish the other guy well. I don't wish he'd die either—

that's usually going too far—but at the least I hope he'll wander around until he needs me again—and I can turn him down.

You can believe all you want that a breakup is clean, but usually there's poison just beneath the surface.

Take Disney chairman Michael Eisner, who may or may not still be running the company when you read this, and the guy he hired in 1995 to be Disney president, Michael Ovitz, the one-time head of the Creative Artists Agency.

These guys were the best of friends for twenty years. Their families vacationed together. When Eisner had his heart bypass operation, Ovitz was the only business associate allowed to visit the hospital. I always thought that since no one could stand either of them, they needed each other to be best friends. My theory about why Eisner hired Ovitz is that Eisner wanted to make sure only he was the most powerful man in show business; what better way than by having the other contender working for him. In any case, when Ovitz came aboard, the town's attitude was "look out world." The combination was rumored to be unbeatable.

Fourteen months later Ovitz was canned. But the biggest controversy was not over his relationship with Eisner, but over Ovitz's huge severance package. Otherwise, although the divorce was as public as it could get, everyone put on their best smile and called it a day.

In February 2004, with forces trying to oust Eisner from running Disney, the truth about his relationship with Ovitz finally came out.

According to the *Los Angeles Times*, Eisner was ready to fire

Ovitz after only five weeks. He kept him on for another year because he thought Ovitz might commit suicide. During that year grace period, the *Times* said Ovitz went through nearly $6 million dollars of personal expenses.

I could go on, but you get the point. When a business partnership breaks up, the parties may say it's really no big deal, they may act like it's no big deal, but it's usually a lie. The truth may stay buried—until it comes out. Don't believe all that you hear.

He F****d Me but Now We're Best Friends Again— Because We *Really* Need Each Other

EVERYONE KIDS ME THAT I have my Hate List, and that the Hate List constantly changes. They're right. There's one network I'd do just about anything to avoid being in business with. The boss is just plain mean, and the chairman is a liar who likes to hurt people for no reason. Twenty years ago it was another network. It's always something, right?

But suddenly I'm doing business today with someone I couldn't stand yesterday.

How can that be?

Sometimes you have to put aside your ego, your personality, and the foul taste in your mouth to work with someone you'd rather never darkened your doorway again. If you're me, you do it only after exhausting every other option and realizing there's no alternative. Ten other people have to pass on my project before I'll go to someone I hate.

If our past dealings weren't especially acrimonious—maybe

we just didn't click—and I just need that person, or he needs me, and it seems like too good an opportunity to pass up, then I hope he's on his best behavior. I keep my eyes wide open, of course. You go where you hoped to never go again because sometimes you can't let a personal grudge or a poor business history put you out of business. That would be stupid. Besides, it's not like being forced to remarry your ex because no one else will have you.

And remember, it's only temporary.

You always run up against people who leave you, who don't like the way you do business, who don't like your ethics, who have a grudge against you. Maybe you put them in a movie that bombed. Maybe they bought a line of clothes from you that flopped. Sometimes you get put into a division that failed. You get promoted to a job that soon gets phased out. The boss sells the company out from under you. Sometimes it's even done maliciously.

When I ran Lorimar Pictures and the company was sold to Warner, Bob Daly, who became my boss, and I had a huge fight over the movie *Penn and Teller Get Killed*. He didn't think it was funny. I thought it was hilarious. Everyone is entitled to their opinion, but walking back to the office from the screening, I lost my temper, and we fought in public. Afterward, in my mind, I thought we'd never talk again. I figured he was going to dump me anyway. In the meantime, I talked about the fight in the press, but when I read the story it made me more angry at myself than at him. His quote was businesslike and patrician, as a leader's should be.

In the end, he didn't dump me. He should have because I

was a pain in the ass, but I walked away, even though to my surprise he tried to keep me.

It took a while for me to realize that my worldview wasn't always correct.

That was years ago. Now whenever we see each other we always shake hands, and say hello. What am I going to do— turn my back?

There are a million reasons to get upset. But in the end, if you let everything that happens in business linger too long you'll end up an angry old man.

Life should be about other things.

I Haven't Heard from Him, He Must Be Doing Well

IF PEOPLE—EVEN FRIENDS—are doing well, they don't usually call to share it. "Hey! Just wanted to let you know that everything's still great!" What can you say to that, especially if your life's not so hot? "Gee, thanks for letting me know." The world can be a selfish place.

Don't take it personally, though. Successful people are busy. Once, they came to you for advice. If what you said helped and they get hot, they suddenly don't have any time left to schmooze. They love you, but they're busy with their own lives. Even my dog only barks when she needs me. I take it for granted my successful friends will call me when they have some time; if I can't wait, I'll call them. Luckily I'm a habitual telephone user at the office. Nothing to be ashamed of.

Mostly, you hear from people when they're in trouble or they want something. This includes not only business associates, acquaintances, and people you've helped before who think you're their mentor, but relatives, ex-wives, and the pool guy.

Sometimes those calls are embarrassing, especially when they come from people who want to be in show business.

I have a friend who, after a marathon TV-watching weekend, called to tell me that there was no reason she couldn't do commercials, and asked if I'd introduce her to a few people. "It's not that hard," she insisted. (Everyone thinks everything everyone else does is a cinch.) I didn't mind helping, even though I knew she was wrong. Getting commercial work is the toughest thing in the world because she'd be up against 100,000 out-of-work actresses who make the rounds every day, everyone knows them, and they're real good at what they do. At least she didn't ask for money, but I've gotten plenty of calls from people who sit at home saying, "I'm a writer," or "I'm an actor," or whatever, but won't hold down a nine-to-five job. When they go broke, they come to me.

Most good actors I know were waiters. Why? Because you never know who you're going to meet in a restaurant. The hours give them plenty of time to do auditions.

My advice: You've got to support yourself while you're chasing your dream.

Then if you get successful and I don't hear from you for a while, I don't mind.

Don't Confuse Business Friends with Real Friends

IMAGINE A GUY HAS a long-standing customer. His biggest customer. He's had this guy locked in for years. Then another guy comes along who has a better product, maybe a better price. Suddenly guy number one is on the outs. Now he has to face his boss, in trouble, and wave his sales projections and bonus good-bye. It's really sad. Everything he counted on when he woke up this morning is no longer there.

After all the explicatives are spoken, one question often remains: "How could he do this to me? We were friends. Good friends."

Not really. Business friendship is exactly what the name implies. You see each other at a party, you say hi. If you call, they'll pick up the phone. Sometimes you go to ball games together, or have barbecues. Maybe you even vacation with your business friends. That seems a lot more intimate than coffee-break gabbing in the lunchroom, but too often these out-of-the-office communal experiences happen because people are afraid to leave their work environment, therefore they take their business with them wherever they go. They're teeing off at the ocean hole of some beautiful Maui golf course while talking about pork belly futures. They can't appreciate a South Pacific sunset and a piña colada without gossiping about who's in and who's about to be canned. You serve a purpose for each other and call it friendship.

But most business-related friendships won't last through a change in position by one party or the other. If you're a buyer and you can't buy anymore, everyone who sent you nice gifts and who took you to lunch will disappear very quickly and go to the next buyer. Which, by the way, I think they should. You know the old saying: "It's not personal. It's business."

You shouldn't be hurt. No one fooled anyone, unless you fooled yourself. The jobs are permanent, the people aren't. I've always said that as long as everyone paid me the money they owed me, all bets are off. I don't remember a time when I called someone I was no longer in business with to have dinner again. Sounds terrible, but when it's over it's over.

If a "friend" you made at work leaves the firm, you may hear from him once or twice the first few weeks, then once a month, then he'll disappear. All that camaraderie is over—until he needs a favor or vice versa. Then you see how much equity exists.

A classic example of business friends is what happens when a movie is shot on location. The work throws together a group of people for months. You become totally involved in each others' lives. You count on each other every day. You may even sleep around. You see your driver at least twice a day, and as with your barber, you tell him everything. But when you've moved on to the next show, how often do you write to each other?

Of course, the problem is that most of the people we know, we know from work. If we make a good connection, we want it to last forever. Who wouldn't want that? But you have to remember it's business, otherwise you'll overestimate your comfort level, break the first rule of business relationships, and spill your troubles. In a business context it's usually taken as a sign of weakness. Expose yourself to family and real friends; otherwise keep on your happy salesman's face.

A real friend is someone who will outlast the business that either of you are in.

Better, they won't be part of your business life at all.

When Your Time Has Come, Success Will Find You

GOOD WORK LEADS TO success. Take a ballplayer who performs brilliantly one season: There's no doubt that he'll get more recognition, more self-confidence, more opportunities, more money—and maybe his picture on a cereal box.

That's easy to understand after the fact. What's tough is being willing to trust that it can happen *before* your success. While you're still on the path. With so many shortcuts and the temptation of easy money, it's tough to be steady and patient and believe in your own instincts.

Jim Henson was offered fortunes to design puppets for advertisers. The advertisers wanted to own the characters but he said no—his rule was "I own everything I do"—and this was when he desperately needed money. But in the end he won because he was right, and made big money from keeping ownership.

Sometimes the waiting period seems endless but if you

believe in your talent you don't have to take the path everyone else took.

It took me twenty-five years to become an overnight success. By then I'd already made good money, but it wasn't until the night the Blues Brothers opened for Steve Martin at the Universal Amphitheater in 1978 that it all came together.

The change happened at the party afterward, at the Victoria Station restaurant. I represented Belushi and Aykroyd. I had *SNL* on the air, and *The Muppet Show*. That night, the Blues Brothers blew everyone away and the head of every studio, record company, network, and whatever stars came, made it their business to meet me. When you're hot—when you've succeeded somehow—the leaders of your industry will seek you out. You won't have to look for them.

It was no mystery why: Everyone figured Belushi and Aykroyd were geniuses, so the guy who represented them must also be a genius, too. I'm not, but I wasn't going to say, "Hey, I had nothing to do with these guys." By keeping quiet, I assumed power. That's another great lesson: Let people talk themselves into what a genius you are. If you can keep your mouth shut, people will assume just about anything.

That night there was so much schmooze swirling around me that even my usual cynicism took a backseat to indulging in the temporary wonderfulness of it all. I didn't want to go home or go to sleep. I was Cinderella with a beard, at the ball, and it was way past midnight.

But the next day I was back to being Bernie again. The party was over and although I had a little more juice in town, I couldn't afford to believe everything from then on would happen just because I snapped my fingers. I still had to stick with the rules and instincts that had gotten me there.

So how do you stand the waiting? Fortunately, "making it" is not always synonymous with money. Nor should it be. There's also personal satisfaction. There's believing that you're doing something for the right reasons, because you'll be able to do better work. There's emotional success. You were first with an idea or product. You knew you knew. It's a good feeling. It will tide you over until the rest comes.

Don't Pet the Snakes

IF YOU USE THE antennae we're all born with you'll figure out quickly which guys in the office, or in life, want to kill you. They have many reasons: They're not as good as you. They're not as smart as you. They're not as handsome as you. They don't have as many friends. Their girls like you. They're paranoid and think you're going to take their place.

Or they're just pricks.

Many pricks are smart enough to hide their prickiness. Others don't, but swear that they'd never do anything bad to you, pal. Don't believe it. Don't pet the snakes. Eventually they'll bite your leg and poison you. Or, to use another analogy: Remember the story of the scorpion and frog? The frog said he'd give the scorpion a ride across the river because the scorpion promised not to sting him. Halfway across the river the scorpion nailed him anyway. When the frog asked why— and mentioned that now they'd probably both drown—the scorpion said, "Sorry. I can't help it. I'm a scorpion."

When someone screws you over for no reason at all, just to say they did it, that's evil. It doesn't have to be to your face. You find out eventually. Someone will call and say, "What does he have against you?"

There are evil people in every business. Power-hungry people. People who want to have the edge. They want to kill you because it makes them more secure—for a second.

When you spot someone evil, stay away from them. Don't court someone whom you know is a miserable pain in the ass. The terrible stories about them are always true. They could be cheap, a liar, neurotic, anything. Don't even meet. Please.

But you meet anyway, right? They represent a lot of money. They're very seductive. You get along and for a moment you think that you're a superhero and you'll show everyone else how good you are. You think, "I can handle this."

Guess what? For a while it will be calm; then hell will break loose again. Why? Evil people never change. Sooner or later the you-know-what hits the fan.

Stay out of the way.

You'll learn.

Let Your Enemy Bury Himself

SOMEONE IN YOUR COMPANY, or maybe in your business, doesn't like you. Whenever he gets a chance, he tries to destroy you. Why you got singled out can be obvious—you're competitors; he thinks you hurt him; he's a mean, ambitious prick—or a mystery. Whatever the reason, you end up spending too much time playing defense and watching your own back. You not only have to focus on your job—and do it well—but you've got to concentrate on staying alive.

This can't go on forever. Should you try to meet with your enemy, talk to the guy, see if you can work it out?

I don't want to go on about Michael Ovitz—he's overdone as a subject, but in this case the facts apply—but at one time we were enemies. Then, one day he called and wanted to make up. He said, "Let's have dinner and straighten this all out. We'll go to Jimmy's Restaurant."

"Fine," I said. I figured enough already.

When I got there I discovered that Ovitz had rented out the

entire party room. It was empty, except that in the middle was a table for two. No one else was around. Immediately I felt strange: There we were, two guys who made our living selling people in show business, sitting down to make peace like it was a *Sopranos* episode. The hubris creeped me out, if you must know the truth. And while we talked a bit about a truce, it hit me that only a fool would expect a man with Ovitz's track record and personality to suddenly change character.

At the time Ovitz was "the most powerful man in Hollywood." Nothing I could do about that except go about my business, work around him, bide my time. Eventually, I figured he'd make a mistake crucial to his downfall. His reputation carried the seeds of his own destruction.

Think about it: If a guy robs seven banks and gets away with it, you know he's going to rob the eighth. If a guy cheats, you know he'll cheat until he gets caught.

I don't feel good about it, but I was right.

Unfortunately, sometimes your enemy may actually succeed in "killing" *you*, but that doesn't change the ultimate outcome. They'll eventually run into someone bigger, try the same tricks, and then get run over. Or the guy will finally have hurt so many people that they come together for the common good and destroy him. I'm picturing a wild crowd, with lanterns and wooden stakes, hunting vampires.

All you have to do is pull up the lounge chair and watch.

Pete Rose is another good example. Rose was probably one of the greatest baseball players who ever lived, if not the greatest. He did everything perfectly. He stole bases, he was a great fielder, he was a great hitter. He also thought he was bigger than the game. For years he just kept pushing his "Pete Rose-ness" in everyone's face, and got away with it, until he brought himself down by gambling. No one tried to destroy him; he did it to himself because he thought he was indispensable. Now that he's finally admitted to betting on baseball, let's hope his future and legacy are brighter.

Let me give you two more names: Richard Nixon. Michael Jackson.

I'm sure you have your own list.

He who believes he can't be destroyed, destroys himself.

Always Trust a Stomachache
and Other Gastrointestinal Warnings

ANY TIME I'M INVOLVED in a project I shouldn't be, or I'm working with someone who is more trouble than he's worth, I get a stomachache. For you it might be a headache, an itch, the shakes, sleepless nights, sexual dysfunction, a literal pain in the ass, or whatever. Don't just brush off the symptoms. Your instinct is using your mind and/or body to warn you. Anything can cause this, from an argument at home to the way people do business. When I was young it came from not getting the woman I wanted. Once, when I was in Vegas taking another $10,000 credit when I didn't have the ten grand to cover it, my stomach *really* hurt. In the office, when someone I don't want to talk to calls, the minute my assistant says the name I feel like throwing up. One of my wives was a constant stomachache—until I left. Or she left me. Doesn't matter: I felt better.

Eventually, I learned to respect the pain as an early warning system. If you're smart, the first two stomachaches should be sufficient. And when you finally tell the problem person, "Look, you and I are getting nowhere. Let's end this thing," you usually don't get much of an argument because they've been having stomachaches, too.

Just Don't Talk Behind My Back in Front of Me

Y OU CAN'T STOP PEOPLE from talking about you behind your back. Or just after you've left the room. Or—sometimes—while you're right in front of them.

The talk takes two forms.

Gossip is a validation of your success, and each success tends to inflate your success—and the gossip. In fact, if you're at all *known*—and I don't mean you have to be a celebrity; any higher-up or standout will do—you should assume people talk about you because they only chatter about what matters to them. If you matter, then you're it.

Cheap talk happens because people read headlines, but not what's underneath them. For instance, people read about my company in the papers and believe I have $200 million in the bank. They treat me with respect—which, by the way, I'm not due, and don't act as if I am—for the wrong reasons.

In truth, I don't have anything close to that kind of money, but if someone wants to believe I'm so wealthy, great. I'm thrilled. Spread the word. It doesn't hurt me to have people think that I don't need them.

Innuendo and backstabbing—the whole dark side of being in an office or a relationship—also comes with the territory. No matter where you are on the food chain, there are always people looking to bring you down.

Should you worry?

Yes. Especially if what people are saying is not true. The trouble with rumors is that if they're repeated enough they become "facts." Perception is reality. Deception is reality, too. It gets into people's heads. A bell once rung is hard to un-ring.

Quick: True or not, what pops into your mind when I say "Michael Jackson"? "George Bush"? "Artificial sweeteners"? "Paris Hilton"? "Pete Rose"? "Hitler"? "Weapons of mass destruction"?

Say there's a rumor that someone I know in the office is getting fired—and it's not true. If I heard it, I'd ask the person who told me, "Who did you hear it from?" Then I'd confront that person, and so forth, until I had tracked it down and killed it. But people rarely do that. Some don't care, some are scared, some are lazy, and the rest actually like hearing bad news about other people. It makes them feel better, which is why rumors like that exist and prosper in the first place.

Sometimes you just have to stand up for yourself and confront backstabbing and betrayal outright.

I once saw a guy who worked in my company having breakfast with one of my enemies. They were at a place I rarely went to, but when I showed up and they saw me, they ran out so fast that by the time the maitre d' sat me in my booth in the back, they were gone. But I spotted something they'd left behind on the table: a gold cigarette lighter. I walked over and grabbed it.

I thought about the situation at breakfast and quickly reached the conclusion that I couldn't let it rest. If someone I counted on was having breakfast with someone on my black-list, then I had a real problem.

I confronted him. He denied being there. "What are you talking about?"

"Here's what I'm talking about," I said, and gave him back his lighter.

He started to scramble: "Oh, we were just talking about how I could make up the differences in our companies."

Right. I figured the other guy was talking trash about me and trying to hire my guy away.

I don't know why he thought he could get away with it in the first place. There's no such thing as a secret in business. There's too much e-mail. Too much overhearing. Too much paper. Too many people know too many things.

Of course, there are times when you confront somebody and they deny it, and there's no way you can get them to admit anything. But you know. And they know you know. And chances are they won't ever do it again—that you know of.

Deliver Bad News Quickly

MOST BUSINESS OPERATES ON the principle that you don't want to deliver bad news, especially in person. No one wants to look anyone in the face and say it's over.

You have to. In fact, *always* give bad news in person, if possible. Give it quickly. Don't sleep on it. Don't figure out how to say it. Blurt it out. We all worry about getting killed, figuratively, but it usually doesn't happen. Quite the opposite, in fact.

In my business, if the head of a network calls me, ninety-nine times out of a hundred it's not to say no. "No" comes from the underlings. And too often they lie in order to soft-pedal it. "You know, we had something just like it in-house."

"We loved it but it didn't test well."

"It would take too long to get started."

"We have nothing to put it with."

It's the same in every business, with slightly different wording.

What about telling the truth: "We don't like it," or "Our needs have changed."

If you're smart enough, you know when you're being lied to. If you're in the middle of making a deal and you hear an obvious whopper, you should say good-bye, pick up your papers, and leave.

When you're waiting for a decision and hear, "We're still thinking about it," it usually means they're stringing you along with hope. *But there is no hope.* They just don't have the balls to say so.

I remember once I wanted to fire someone. I worried it to death. I thought about the guy's family and imagined how his face would look when I gave him the news. Every time I saw him I lied and said all was well. The anticipation only made it worse; I got an anxious stomach, diarrhea. Eventually, I forgot the original reason I wanted to fire the guy. Then I almost forgot to fire him. In fact, I waited four months before I finally called him in. By then I'd planned my speech and even rehearsed it. But the first words out of my mouth were: "So, where are you going to work next?"

Yikes! Sue me; it just slipped out. To his credit, he said, "Oh, thank God you finally told me." He knew. He was so glad to hear it, and I felt like an idiot.

No Call Is the Same As Calling to Say No

SAY YOU WROTE A screenplay or a novel and sent it to an agent. Or you're trying to get into business with someone, they've got your proposal, and you're just waiting for a decision. Six months have passed, you've called or e-mailed ten times, and you still haven't heard back.

Is no call the same as saying no?

Unfortunately, yes.

To those who have to make decisions: You've got to learn how to *say* no when you mean no. It's terrible to not call, not to mention not be called. No one has the right to play with another person's mind. Who are you not to respond? If you don't want to bother reading some material, or making a deal, mail the material back right away and say, "I'm not going to look at it." If you look, be courteous enough to answer quickly.

By the way, this doesn't happen only at the beginning of the process. I know of ten TV shows that have been off the air and out of production for three years, yet no one ever actually picked up the phone to officially say, "You're canceled."

I don't care what business you're in; no one is that busy. It's manners, manners, manners. If someone took the time to write something or present an idea, and you don't want to be involved, make the call.

You don't wait to call to say yes, do you?

Disney chairman Michael Eisner, who has his share of faults, still handles this situation the best way I've seen. He takes your letter/proposal/whatever and dashes off a two-line answer right on it. It's his handwriting. It's personal. It's quick. You know he saw what you sent. Even though he very rarely says "Yes," it's a great system. Whoever taught it to him was really smart.

Learn how to say "no" and maybe you'll stay in business long enough to say "yes," and have it mean something.

Let the Guy Who's Paid to Decide, Decide

GUYS LIKE ME ARE paid a lot of money to make decisions. There are lots of reasons: I believe in myself and am willing to take risks. I've shown that I can learn from my successes and failures because I pay attention to what works. I don't simply copy someone else's success or try some half-assed idea I once had over and over while hoping for different results. That's the definition of insanity.

So how come guys like me, or anyone in a position to make major business decisions, also need a group of strangers to tell us if we're right or wrong?

I'm not talking about the audience or the customer.

I'm talking about marketing focus groups.

"Testing" is a ubiquitous evil and, frankly, I don't expect it to stop. But if I'd listened to all the advice and predictions I've heard over the years I'd probably have gone broke instead of being able to write this book.

I operate on instinct. I do what seems like a good idea at

ᴜᴉe time, based on years of experience. I don't need to be second-guessed. What does a cross section of citizens know about how everyone else will respond? Statistics lie and focus groups guess wrong as often as they guess right. So why spend all that money on even odds?

Here's why: Companies test-market and consult focus groups to buy deniability and to shirk responsibility for a failure. "We really loved it, but it tested poorly." Unfortunately, there's no book in which you turn to Chapter 4, page 7 and read: "Here's what you do now . . ." All the test data in the world doesn't add up to a good screenplay, TV show, automobile, investment product, or bar of soap. We're all going to make great choices and big mistakes. Why not make them your own? In this world you have to bet on yourself.

You also have to trust the people who work for you to do their jobs.

If I pay someone a million dollars to write a book, I take it for granted she's going to write a great book. In fact, the best book I could get for a million dollars. I'm not just a fool with money to burn; I did some research, asked around about good writers, read something she'd written before. When we met I felt a personal connection. Maybe I'm wrong, but after I pay the million am I now going to tell the gal *how* to do her job?

In TV, writers on the exclusive list of trusted writers get lots of money to come up with show ideas. But then they have to submit the script to the network, and listen to twelve executive bozos who could never get a job writing, tell them what's wrong with it. Next, a dozen marketing bozos explain why it will or won't sell.

The emotion driving all this is fear. Do the network bozos really want to make the script better? No. They want to make it palatable and easy for their boss to understand. God forbid they hand in something really *different*. They'll get killed immediately. Ninety-nine out of a hundred times the suits will say, "That'll never work." Why? *Because it hasn't worked before*. Makes you want to kill yourself when that happens, no matter what business you're in.

You can't, of course. New ideas have to come from someplace.

To be honest, it's not always a corporate lack of imagination or inherent fear of trying something different. Some executives *want* to go against the grain, but the thought of getting in trouble for doing something outside the norm is scary. They spend more time protecting their jobs than going on the line for a creative concept they believe in because they're in temporary jobs. The company may be sold tomorrow or may not be number one at the end of the ratings period. The boss who hired them may be out of a job, and that means they'll probably be out, too.

If I'd tried to play it safe there might never have been a *Muppet Show*, an *ALF*, a *Love Connection*, a *Saturday Night Live*, a *Hee Haw*, a *Dangerous Liaisons*. (I like to think I played a crucial part in getting each off the ground.) You may think of some as schlock and others as culturally groundbreaking—and I may agree—but in the end it doesn't really matter. They are what they are, and they have two things in common: I stood behind them, and they were all hits.

It's Not Over Until You Walk out the Door

I ONCE SPOKE TO a client who thought his TV show was on the rocks and about to be canceled. I'd heard murmurs, so it was more than just the usual Hollywood fear factor, but we'd been told nothing definite, so it was business as usual. His anger and disappointment didn't surprise me, but something else I detected in his voice did: Even though the show would for the moment go on, he had already left it behind in his head. I could tell his heart was no longer part of the equation, either. I knew he'd just go through the motions until the end came.

That's dangerous. No matter what happens at work, you have to remain a professional. If you've been fired, or even if you know you'll quit tomorrow, you have to do the best job you can until you actually walk out the door. Believe me, you never know who's watching you. If someone from the next place you work calls for a recommendation, having your former boss say, "He's great. We were downsizing. I hated to let him go, but I had to, but he's a professional and gave a hundred percent until the end," is far better than the alternative.

When I knew I was going to leave William Morris, I kept it secret, and worked for every client until the day I left to become a manager. I took no one with me. A few months later—with perfect timing because I was down in the dumps and really needed it—Jim Henson called and said that he wanted me to be his manager. Imagine if I'd let his interests slide just because I knew I wouldn't be around much longer. That relationship lasted from 1964 until the day he died.

There were times at *Saturday Night Live*, when Lorne Michaels could have slacked off. Between fights with the network, and the press regularly declaring the show *Saturday Night Dead*, he could easily have thought, *Why bother?* Instead, Lorne worked harder. He's had his ups and downs, and even left the show for five years. But they asked him back, and soon the show will have been on air for thirty years.

Jack McKeon came aboard as manager of the Florida Marlins in an interim capacity in early 2003, when the team's record was three losses and one win. He could have said, "Hey, I'm seventy-two. I'll just dial it in until the season's over." After all, these were the Marlins, not the Yankees. The media didn't care. Instead, McKeon worked hard and tried to mold the team. His unquenchable spirit and enthusiasm infected all the players. They won the World Series.

Imagine being in a Broadway show. Your yearlong run starts out fantastically. The excitement and the adrenaline are pumping. Then there's a bad review in the *Los Angeles Times*. But the show is still sold out, and you have to perform eight times a week. Eventually, the audience dwindles a bit. Maybe the cast is never as good as you thought it would be when you signed on. What do you do?

Whether you're the star of the show or a chorus member you have to stay steady.

As long as you're at the job, do the job you're being paid to do.

Sometimes the Only Way to Get Ahead Is to Leave the Company

A FTER YOU'VE SERVED YOUR apprenticeship at your first job, take a look at yourself and assess what you've learned. Then look around and assess future opportunities and challenges. If you like it, stay where you are. If you discover that your original ideas are consistently better than the company you're in, and your bosses don't believe in your full potential—or that there are too many other employees ahead of you in line waiting for *their* potential to be explored—maybe it's time to leave.

There's nothing to feel bad about. Leaving is not disloyal—unless you're constantly chasing a fatter paycheck and have trouble sticking around *anywhere* long enough. There's something wrong with a full-time job–hopper because if you can't find your place after one or two other jobs, I think you'd better change businesses.

I think of moving on under your own steam like being traded in sports, only you're trading yourself. Some teams, no matter how great, may not have a use for your particular kind of player. But on another team, a player like you becomes a star. Why? Because the new team—or the new company—functions differently.

They're willing to give you a leg up instead of holding you by the leg.

In my case, I started at the William Morris Agency. Pretty soon I thought I was smarter than everyone around me. I stuck it out, moved up the ladder slowly but surely, but soon discovered that I didn't fit naturally into the company style. I left because the boss, who didn't believe in my potential, thought I was too rebellious. I thought he was a stick-in-the-mud.

I'm not complaining by the way. Years ago William Morris's rigidity accounted for both its stability *and* it's inability to evolve quickly and respond to new marketplace situations. Every time I wanted to try something new I was told it couldn't be done; for instance, before it became big business, I wanted us to represent professional athletes. Believe me, this problem isn't exclusive to Hollywood.

By the way, I wasn't alone in realizing I had to move on. David Geffen, Barry Diller, the five guys who started Creative Artists Agency, Jerry Seinfeld's managers George Shapiro and Howard West, and producer/director Irwin Winkler, to name a very few from my era, also left. For years others followed.

My next job was with a little management company. I was an equal partner, but financially the poor relation. After a couple years they sent me from New York to Los Angeles to start the West Coast office. Our philosophy had always been to sign stars. That was fine in New York when we were all together. But in Los Angeles, I asked myself why would any star want to

be with me? It's not like I knew anyone, or that we had a heavy enough roster to attract other big names.

At first I tried to toe the line. I had lunch with Jack Palance, a big star then (his last big role was in the *City Slickers* movies—and he did those famous one-handed push-ups at the Oscars). We ate at the Brown Derby restaurant. Throughout our two-hour meal I was in great form. Finally, Palance said, "Bernie, I really like you. You're terrific. But what can you do for me?"

I was honest. "Absolutely nothing."

Palance laughed like hell, and with what seemed like affection said, "You're right."

What could I do that he couldn't do himself? He already got all the best scripts. Maybe I could hold his jacket when he stood up.

Desperation sometimes leads to creativity, so I changed tactics. Instead of pursuing big stars I went after writers, directors, composers, and choreographers. I didn't exactly leave my company, but I changed the direction on my end—which, since I was out in Los Angeles by myself, was like leaving to start something new. Little did I know that within three years the people I'd gone after would be the most important people in television, and hold all the power.

Trying new tactics took me into new and better worlds. I started making more money. Too bad my partners in New York didn't appreciate it, so I left the company to start my own business—and took my clients.

That was the last move I made. I found a situation in which my talent was appreciated, even if I had to appreciate it myself. All it took was the courage to move on.

The Best Way to Take Failure and Rejection Is to Wallow in It

I HATE FAILURE AND rejection. Who doesn't? Whether my client's show got canceled, or a woman I liked was for some mysterious reason not attracted to me, I always felt like *I* did something wrong. Some people work overtime to ignore the bad feelings—push them down, buck up, put on a happy face—but that's never worked for me. I wish I could make myself rejection proof, but short of that I'd settle for not feeling like a putz forever.

In the early sixties, when I quit being an agent at William Morris and became a partner in a management firm, I was hardly an instant success. I'd left with no clients and, after weeks of making lists and watching shows, I still had none. Some people can pick up the phone and make cold calls, but I've never been able to do that—which also explains why I never had any luck meeting women in bars. (Introduce me first and I'm great.)

So there I'd sit at my desk with absolutely nothing to do,

rooting for lunch to come early. Even that could be unpleasant. Sometimes my partner and I would eat at the New York Friars Club, where I'd look at all the comedians and wish they were my clients. But I couldn't face the rejection of asking and being turned down.

My solution to this paralysis was to make an invisible appointment every day, at four o'clock, and go home and get into bed. On Fridays I left at two o'clock. I was so depressed that I'd hide under the covers and put myself "on ice," and not leave my apartment until Monday.

Ironically, that seemed to help. Lying around got so boring that I'd turn my situation over and over in my head and sink deeply into analzying all I'd done and didn't do. Maybe I wasn't as good as I thought I was. Maybe I'd gotten carried away with the idea of being a manager and should have stayed at my old job. Maybe I should sell hats. Depressing. When that got boring I'd come to the conclusion that maybe I'd done everything I could to make things work, the past was past, and I simply had to try again.

On Monday morning I'd come into the office with a "Yeah, let's go!" attitude.

Sometimes that attitude would even last until Tuesday.

Eventually, I got back to my life, a little wiser and stronger—and better equipped to handle the next brush-off.

We all have occasional bad days and bad luck, but when it happens consistently, sneaks into and takes root in your head, you go into a slump. I don't know what turns a few disappointments into a full-fledged slump, or how quickly (which comes first: the chicken or the slump?), I just know that suddenly I don't care about anything: diet, exercise, work, family, sex, etc.

I've had slumps all my life. In fact, I'm in a slump right now. Seriously. I didn't want to get out of bed this morning, but I forced myself to come into the office. Thank goodness I've been around long enough to have learned how to fake being the usual "public me" enough to ward off annoying attempts to cheer my mood, like, "At least you don't have cancer." Or, "Be glad you're not poor."

Okay, so compared to the rest of the world my slumps are horseshit. But when you're in a slump, you're in a slump.

Worse is when a slump leads to a slump leads to a slump. Once the introspection starts I'm on the downhill slide. For some people, it's a long trip. They do things to hurt themselves, from staying in bed for a week, to doing drugs. Or hanging themselves—which is *really* a slump.

Fortunately, I realized early in my career that for me to get over my slumps I had to wallow in them. That means accepting I'm in one in the first place. To deal with any emotional challenge, I have to go through the fire, not around it. I don't mean that I make a pain in the ass of myself; I don't keep moaning, "Those stupid bastards." And I try not to make everyone else in my life feel as pathetic as I do.

Soon I can start getting better. I try to remember the times I was riding high. Go for a walk, change my eating habits, do positive activities. I'm waiting for that *click!* that says "Okay, things are looking up." It doesn't happen overnight. (And no good news is so good to snap me out of a slump immediately.) My body needs to deslumpisize itself.

Here's the good news about slumps: They're the same whether you're thirty or seventy, only the older you get the more you realize that the slump will end. It will pass, even though when you're in the middle of a slump it feels like it's permanent.

Hey, it could be worse: At least you're not like some ballplayer who's gone 0 for 40 in front of thousands of fans. And if you are, you'll get over it.

Don't Confuse Ego with Self-Confidence

E GO CAN BE A terrible thing. If you have too much ego, you think your shit doesn't stink. But if you have too little ego, then everyone dumps on you. If you have the right amount of ego, you will flow through life a little more easily. I guess ego is a lot like Goldilocks in the three bears' house: An uninvited guest just trying to find the comfort zone.

The guy who sells to JCPenney has an ego because he has a relationship with the buyer. He walks in like he owns JCPenney. But if he pushes that ego too far, the buyer will shut off and the salesman will no longer have a right to his ego. Ego shouldn't be obvious. People shouldn't know you feel that you have them in the bag. Look how Vegas operates: "Hit me. Hit me again."

"Yes, sir. Yes, sir."

The dealer is probably rooting for you to die every time, but you wouldn't know it in a million years. He's a professional. He'll keep a straight face. The pit boss will look you straight in the eye. He knows you're a bust-out but he won't let you know he knows. It's all a game. A beautiful woman walks into a room and crosses her legs, making her skirt a little higher. It's not an obvious move; it just goes with her persona. But you notice. And she knows it.

Some people say you need a tremendous ego to get anywhere in the world. I think you need a tremendous amount of *self-confidence*. There's a difference. The latter is knowing your powers and using them accordingly. Ego is blindly thinking you can do it all.

Unfortunately, there are few ego balancers in my business. Maybe box office, but that doesn't always work. Certainly not critics; no one pays attention.

It took a while, but these days I'm self-confident, like San Francisco Giants slugger Barry Bonds when he walks to the plate. I haven't always been. There was a time when I wouldn't miss any chance to be seen in public: Emmys, Oscars, screenings, concerts, charity events, whatever. Turn on a light and I'd be there. It was very important to me to be accepted as part of the establishment. I met Hollywood players, talked to them, made sure they knew who I was.

In the late seventies everyone finally did, and my ego flew out of bounds. I had *The Muppet Show*—it was number one. I had *Saturday Night Live*. I had the Blues Brothers. And I represented John Belushi. Earlier, I had actually invented *Hee Haw*, but I thought I had invented show business.

I spent two months being a total putz. I was a forty-eight-year-old man wearing stupid silk jackets that said "Blues Brothers" or "The Muppet Show." When my clients performed I'd walk up and down the theater aisles to make sure everyone knew I was the manager and the producer—a big shot. Then, one evening in New York, on my way out the apartment door, I looked in the hallway mirror and here's what I saw: a fat guy wearing a Blues Brothers hat, a Blues Brothers scarf, Blues Brothers Ray-Ban sunglasses, and a Blues Brothers button ("On A Mission From God") on a blue silk Blues Brothers jacket. Then my wife said out loud exactly what I was thinking: "Bernie, you're a schmuck."

To tell you the truth, I sort of knew it, but I was having too good a time. When you wait so long to become an overnight success, I think you're allowed a few months of self-delusion and schmuckiness—but that's about it. I didn't hurt anyone. My ego abused mostly myself. At least I didn't walk into restaurants and demand tables, or tell anyone, "Don't you know who I am?"

If you ever have to ask that question, *you're no one*.

The Other Guy's Not As Smart
As Either of You Think He Is

WHEN I STARTED OUT in business I thought everyone above me was smarter than I was because I couldn't have had a more grunt position—the mailroom. After a couple weeks I realized that the guys in the mailroom weren't any smarter; but then I looked at the guys who'd gotten out of the mailroom and thought, if only because they were out, that they must be really smart. When I finally got out I revised that opinion. As an assistant I thought all the lower-rung executives must be geniuses—until I became one. Then I analyzed which ones might be vulnerable because they weren't as bright as I'd given them credit for being. When I moved to a higher level executive . . . Well, you get the picture: The game goes on and on. Even when you're the boss, you can still think someone else is smarter than you because he's a bigger boss. Or has a better golf handicap. Or two planes.

It's got nothing to do with smarts, only perspective—or worse. You'd like to think that smarts is what it takes to rise up, but often it's dumb luck. Or a personality disorder: Narcissism is a good one. I can name five major self-obsessed bastards who are more successful than I'll ever be. I also know that for every guy like that who makes it, thousands don't. Thank goodness.

Just because someone's got more money than you doesn't make him better.

Don't be blinded by a hotshot. Don't think you're not as good because most of the time they aren't either. Spend too much time looking at someone else's success and asking yourself what they have that you don't have, and you only short-change yourself. It's not about who drives the coolest car. They could spend most of their money on car payments and be living on fast food. She could be a bust-out gambler who just had a good week. Maybe he's just a con man who thinks he is so smart that no one will con him. Good luck. His time will come. The easiest person to con is a con man.

Don't underestimate people either. Some actually are pretty smart, and if they do something great, give credit. Try to figure out what else is in their bag of tricks. Take a look in yours. Respect what they do, and if the opportunity comes up, do the smart thing and work with them in any capacity. Make it your job to learn what you can without threatening them. It's better to be part of a winning formula than all of a losing one.

If you're at the top, lots of guys will want to take your place. Find the one who really gets what you do, who has a vision, and, most of all, never be afraid of someone who reminds you of yourself.

Leaders Don't Always Have to Be Assholes

IF SOMEONE WHO WORKS for you has a problem—either personal or professional or both—they have to feel like they can bring it to you. You *want* to be the guy who everyone feels free to talk to. If you're not you won't know everything that's going on. I believe it's better to know than to not know, and to accomplish that you have to actually be willing to listen to people.

The instinct that connects you to the basic concerns of your employees is what makes a good leader.

Sometimes, even if I'm not feeling particularly open—say I'm just not in the mood— I'm still too scared to not know everything that's going on. So I put on an act and feign interest simply for my own survival. Eventually my mood improves and I've got the info I need as well.

Some leaders aren't accessible. They think being remote and secretive makes them more powerful, and often it does for a time. And what they do know they don't share. The door is always closed.

But here's the other side: Look what happened to Richard Nixon. He was a peculiar duck. People were scared of him. No one wanted to bring him bad news. Everything was filtered through an inner circle. The people who worked for him didn't tell him everything, and they kept others away as well. Eventually, that's what brought Nixon down because when it was time to save himself he couldn't; he didn't know what had gone on. And if he did, he didn't know what his underlings had done to cover it up.

The more you know the more you can protect yourself — and keep from getting in trouble in the first place.

I have seen so many people put themselves out of business by becoming the "act on the hill" that surround themselves with employees who only say yes. Look at Michael Jackson. He's got so many sycophants feeding him horseshit that he doesn't even know he has problems. Better to be honest and let people help you fix things. Look at all these CEOs and big businesses that cooked the books and went broke. No one wanted to say, "My God, we're in trouble."

And when someone did, no one wanted to pay attention. Or they got fired.

Most successful people are ingratiatingly open (and, when they have to be, completely secretive). I'm always shocked at how much information people actually carry. Eventually they have to unload it. If you're the first person they see and you're open and they know you won't use it against them, you'll know everything that's going on.

I have always been accessible. In high school I knew every-thing about the people I hung out with because they'd call me first. Listening came naturally to me. I wasn't the leader of the pack, but *I was the one most willing to be in the game.* I'm basically a problem fixer. I say, "Come here, let me put my arm around you. I understand." It comes from watching my father, who was president of our synagogue. He was like a ward healer. He'd say, "I birth them, bar mitzvah them, and I bury them."

A hundred times a year people in the office ask my assistant if they can have five minutes with me. They're either going to tell me they're leaving, they're not getting ahead quickly enough, or ask if I can help them with something.

True leadership is in part predicated on having been one of — and in some ways *still* being one of — those you're leading. Lee Iacocca could walk down the assembly line at the auto plant and do every job. A good TV or movie producer or show runner can do every job on the set. General George Patton was a good leader in World War II because he scared the shit out of his men, he got them to do the job they had to do, and he knew in his heart how they suffered. He would fight along with them until he was told not to.

A good leader is also inspiring. In baseball he's the guy who always tries to take the extra base. In hockey he's the guy who will start the fight on the ice. In basketball he's the guy they give the ball to with three seconds left.

The leader isn't perfect but he's the guy who doesn't choke.

Most people run away from being that guy.

A good leader wants to be that guy.

Some leaders employ fear or arrogance. They think they're better than everyone else. But just because you're going up the ladder doesn't mean you're associating with a better class of people. It's easy to meet shitheads who are higher up and richer than you. People who, like Groucho Marx said, don't want to belong to any club that will take them. That attitude works for a time, but not forever. If Martha Stewart were nicer—or the public and private perception of her was more positive—does anyone think she'd have had the trouble she had? A lot of people do questionable things, but when I see the authorities go after them I wonder if it's not really their own fault. Set yourself up as an inaccessible separatist and when you make a mistake you learn the real meaning of *alone*.

I've always found that the really successful leaders were guys I could talk to. Take Wally Jordan. At the William Morris Agency in the fifties, he was a supreme packager of television. Every day at the close of business he would call in his three top agents—they handled ABC, NBC, and CBS—and put a bottle of scotch on the table and say, "Tell me what happened today, guys."

Each evening the knowledge flowed to him from the field as he sat there like a general surrounded by lieutenants. Then he would call the heads of all the networks and disseminate his info about what the others were doing as he saw fit. Being open made him king.

Don't Be Afraid of Fear

WE LIVE IN A climate of fear, from the very important (national security), to the ridiculous (show business). Anyone who tells you they don't live with constant anxiety is full of it.

Take my business. The writer: "Will they like my script?" The agent: "Will the client be happy?" The manager: "Oh my God, what will I do? He's not happy; he didn't get the job." The lawyer: "I couldn't negotiate for the bigger trailer on the set." The director: "Will the studio like my cut?" The producer: "Will I ever work with this studio again?"

There's never been a day I've walked into my office when I haven't been afraid. Everyone in business is insecure. I get anxious every morning that whatever I have will all go away because I guessed completely wrong on some crucial decision. My greatest fear has been with me since I saw *Death of a Salesman* as a kid. It made a huge impression. Willy Loman was loyal to the firm for thirty-odd years and then they just dumped him. I never wanted to be fifty-five or sixty and have to go looking for a job. That's one reason I went into business on my own: Better to be an owner than to depend on someone else to have your best interests at heart.

It may seem ironic but fear has helped make me successful. I know it's there in just about every situation, and I can use it to my advantage. It's part of why I'm good at what I do. I'm always ready for the you-know-what to hit the fan. That's why every time the phone rings I don't jump out of my seat with worry because I long ago learned that people don't call me just to say "How are ya?" I call them to say that; they call because there's a problem. That's what I do for a living.

Some people use fear to get ahead.

Abe Lastfogel, the grand old man of the William Morris Agency, loved this very simple line when someone gave him a hard time: "I'll deal with your successor." He was rarely mistaken.

Lew Wasserman, who ran MCA/Universal, was an imposing guy in both size and reputation. He could come off like your uncle and be the nicest guy in the world—unless you screwed up and he had to scream at you, which he was regularly known to do. Sometimes he screamed just to keep you in your place.

Michael Ovitz, trying to live up to his reputation as a powerful and influential guy, tried to copy Wasserman's style. But he did it clumsily.

Everyone in the business knew about Lew's temper. The message was out there: "Don't fuck with Lew." Same with Ovitz. But if Wasserman wanted to punish you, he did it without you directly knowing that he had. All of a sudden an opportunity would dry up, a deal would go south. He wielded his power and the fear that went with it in a smooth, elegant, and—believe it or not—tactful way. Ovitz employed overt thuggism. He threw haymakers, and uppercut punches. He told you that you should fear him. He talked about it. Not Wasserman, who, by the way, had 1,400 people at his funeral.

We're all animals in the jungle. Whatever your business, the idea is to survive. But how? By our plumes or our claws? Wasserman scared the hell out of me, but I also copied his style. I developed a persona that looks to everyone as if nothing often bothers me. When something does bother me, I lose my mind for five minutes and it has a ripple effect. Word spreads and the rumor/knowledge that I might have a temper—in other words, "don't get Bernie mad"—becomes more valuable than actually *losing* my temper. It's a game. Most people think I'm much tougher than I've actually had to be. And that's just the way I like it.

Nothing Is Brain Surgery
Except Brain Surgery

Y OU MAY LOVE WHAT you do for a living, but don't overrate it. No matter how aggressively you pursue your job, or how much you adore it, try not to feel too self-important. How you negotiated a deal is really boring. The TV star you met over rubber chicken at the charity dinner is just an actor. You may be hot, you may be cold. Even if you mess up a big deal, it's not life and death. You may have to find a new job, but life goes on.

Make a mistake with brain surgery and it's over.

I'm not saying it's not easy to lose your way. I lost perspective when I had big hits with the Blues Brothers and the Muppets. And I know there are heavy jobs in our business — studio head, network boss. Those guys have a great deal of power. Some take it very seriously, and that's great as long as it's the job they take seriously, not themselves. Like the American Indians who say that no one owns the land, we're just minding it for future generations: The big job will always be there; you just inhabit it temporarily.

Unfortunately, some people change overnight when they get a big position. In my experience that means they'll lose the position sooner rather than later. In fact, you can count on it. Then they'll go back to being the nice guy they were before, but now it's too late. For instance, a friend of mine went from being a big lawyer in town to being a studio head, at the same time I also moved up to studio head. All of a sudden he stopped being friendly with me. When I asked why he told me, "You're my competition now." Maybe I changed a bit, too, but mostly I kept my cool because I understood that everyone was suddenly so nice to me because I controlled the purse strings. It's not that they thought I had become a better quality person overnight.

Eventually, my friend and I both lost our jobs. But we were never close friends again.

The other part of this is to not take things so seriously that you forget about real life in the meantime. Too many people put their work way above their family. They think they'll always have time for their family. But business—any business— is not as important as life. It may sound obvious, but if it was, people would act differently.

Home is reality. Home is a wife or husband, and maybe kids.

We all have our excuses. Mine was that I wanted badly to get ahead. Some people do that by working late. I needed to establish an identity. I had to go to Vegas with a client. I was scared to miss an opening or a party or a charity event because, my goodness, how could they hold an affair without me? And maybe I'd get my picture in the *Hollywood Reporter* or *Daily Variety* or the newspaper. My ego was at stake.

At home my kids would say, "You never drive us to school" as I headed out the door to a breakfast meeting. My only answer was, "I know. I'm too busy paying for the school."

Eventually I'd been to every dinner, to every TV show taping, to every movie premiere and cocktail party. I finally realized that if I didn't go to another function no one would miss me — and they'd still know who I was. Better to be home eating a tuna fish sandwich and watching sports on TV, or taking my family to the movies.

First It's About the Idea, Then It's about the Money

WHEN I STARTED OUT I was as broke as anyone. Did I envy the people with money? Sure. I'm still envious, only now it's of guys who have their own planes. I know what it's like; when I ran Lorimar Pictures I had *two* planes.

I didn't start out in business to have a plane, or for that matter, to pile up the money. I had an idea to do something I loved, and to find my place in that world.

Babe Ruth didn't play because of the money; there was no money then. In fact, ask yourself if a big, ungainly guy like the Babe could be a ballplayer today. Hardly a chance.

Why does Roger Clemens pitch in his forties? Sure, the money is good, but pitching is his identity.

Actors might dream of making $20 million a picture, but they start out as waiters, knowing it takes luck and drive to last long enough just to get to the middle of the pack. Most actors become semi-stars, semi-names. They could do something else, but they stick around because they love what they do.

Many innovators keep at it because they do what they do for the thrill of it all, not the thrill of having it all. When the original guys—Bill Paley (CBS) and Robert Sarnoff (NBC)—ran the networks, it was because they were trailblazers who loved the communications business. Steve Jobs may be riding high today on Apple's iPod and Pixar (not to mention being resurrected at Apple), but in the beginning it was just him and Steve Wozniak building the Apple Computer prototype in a garage.

Once upon a time, Wolfgang Puck was a chef at Ma Maison in West Hollywood. Now everyone knows his restaurants, packaged foods, and frozen pizzas.

Jim Henson started with a green felt frog.

Real Men Get Nervous

ANY SMART GUY, WHEN he makes a big deal, gets nervous. You thought he gets happy and celebrates? Well, maybe for a few minutes. Then he gets nervous, and for good reason. He's wondering if the work will be worth the effort. He wonders if he can keep his boss happy. He's anxious that just because he succeeded before, doesn't mean he will this time.

When I sell a television show I have that moment of, "Oh, my God, I sold it!" I'm elated. Next comes the hugs, kisses, and PR announcements. Then I realize: A hundred new people are going to come into my life with a hundred new problems each, and I'm going to have to solve every damn one of them. Man, that's scary. Good thing I like my work.

Everyone thinks making the big score makes all your problems disappear. Wrong. The only reason people look so calm and cool in the newspaper stories is because the portrait photographer made sure they looked that way. As soon as the session's over they go back to worrying—if they're any good.

What does every network head do every morning? They scan the ratings numbers. Every Saturday morning every actor/director/producer looks at the early edition to see if their movie is going to be in the theaters *next* Saturday. Every boss of every company looks at the sales figures.

To calm my nerves I often make light of a success and say, "I fooled them again." It took years before I could admit to myself, "I must know *some*thing. I can't have faked it for this long." But even so I still get anxious, and I'm glad for it. If you don't worry, you're a putz.

Keep the Odds Even and You Might Survive

I F I PROMISE TO fix you up on a date with a woman so beautiful that you'll faint, I've already stacked the odds against her
and chances are you'll be disappointed. Unless she's a fashion
model—and who is, besides a fashion model—she can't possi-
bly live up to your expectations or my hype. If I were her,
especially with me as an advance man, I'd start worrying. And
maybe you should, too.

Great expectations can fool you into thinking the reality
will match. Look how it works in television: Every year the
networks hold an event called the "up fronts," when they
announce to the advertisers what's going to be on the air next
year. Out of these five or six days of chaos come the early
favorites, based on advertisers' and media analysts' response.
And, of course, the producers of whichever show nabbed the
time period after a big hit (e.g., *Friends*) is bragging, "I'm
made. I am golden."

Most years, this new "guaranteed hit" fails. And not necessarily because it's bad—though it often is. Here's the problem: The minute people's hopes are pinned on you, the price of poker gets higher. If you come out of the box with an okay or better-than-okay number, they're already disappointed. It's like if the New York Yankees don't win the pennant every year: The owner runs around saying, "You guys are bums." In 2003 the Yankees lost the World Series in the seventh game. I'd take that for my team.

Overcooked expectations can turn a quiet double into a resounding out. I've made a lot of money with quiet doubles. I'd rather slip in gently. I'll take the good time slot and bet that, given time to grow under the light of less glaring expectations, viewers will find me. When they see the show I'll be happy if they judge it based on their experience instead of what they've been told or conditioned to expect in advance.

This applies across the board: to cars, medicines, vacations, toothpaste, restaurants, breakfast cereal, and the new wonder widget you just created at your company.

I'm not saying it's bad to get excited. Just don't get too excited. The difference is just a little bit. A shade. A hair. But it's the difference that counts.

It's not easy, I know. Hype and inflated expectations are everywhere. It's worse than rush hour traffic. We live in the headline generation because nowadays it's about the only way to get attention. Like the kid in class who raised his hand all the time—saying, "Call on me!"—anyone with something to promote is screaming, "Look at me!"

The intensity of hype grows in proportion to scarcity of attention. Things can really get out of hand. Smart people don't believe the hype about themselves or others. An alarm goes off. They make up their own minds and get a little nervous if someone likes . . . or hates . . . something too much. Remember James Cameron's *Titanic*?

"It's a bomb. Don't go near it."

"Cost $200 million; Jim Cameron really blew it this time."

Turned out to be one of the biggest hits of all time.

Talent Only Sleeps, It Never Dies

THIS IS VERY IMPORTANT and I don't have to be long-winded about it: Very talented people sometimes make horrible choices or have terrible luck. But if you believe in someone, if your instinct says the person is not only hot but good, then a failure or an idea poorly executed is not the end of the world.

Take my client Rob Lowe. He'd had a few rocky years and had played Prince Charming in a skit at the Academy Awards—and it fell flat. He was still the exact same talented actor, the same good-looking guy, but despite good notices in movies, he was off Hollywood's radar.

He came to me through Lorne Michaels, who needed to hire a celebrity who didn't cost an outrageous amount of money, for a part in *Wayne's World 2*. We had a meeting and I suggested Rob. I didn't represent him at the time; I was just a fan. And I believed in him.

Lorne loved the idea, Rob worked out, the movie scored.

One day, Rob and his wife were at my house with Lorne. We were playing tennis, and Rob asked if I'd represent him. I said sure.

Our first discussion was about how to overcome any perception problems he'd acquired. By the way, this was no surprise to Rob; he knew it and was ready. The plan was to keep working whenever possible, little by little. *Wayne's World 2* gave us a boost, and Rob moved into independent films, a TV movie, theater. He worked again with Mike Myers on *Austin Powers*, and all of a sudden the perception of Rob changed. And then, due to his hard work, along came the part of Sam Seaborn on *West Wing*. Who knew it would be such a big hit or bring such respect and attention to Rob, but that's what we'd been waiting for. Six months later he was hot again and became a big, big television name.

Another example: Travolta and Bruce Willis in *Pulp Fiction*. Both careers, particularly Travolta's, benefited. And they could pull it off because the rule holds: Talent doesn't disappear; sometimes it just naps for a while.

By the way, I take my own advice. I just spent a couple years working on a bunch of TV shows. At the outset, I was ecstatic at selling three in one season. Now they've all gone south. Sure I'm disappointed, but like playing golf, you can't think about the shot you just missed; you have to think about the next one. Now I'm telling myself, "I've got to do it again." I have to because the people who can go back and do it again are the ones who make it. Eventually, I'll get lucky.

Say you're in a situation around the office. You were once a hotshot but things have been cool for a while. What do you do? Easy: Stick with yourself. The right opportunity will come again and if you're truly talented you'll grab it and shine. All you have to do is to keep working. It's like we say in show business: No one will ever (re)discover you if you just sit in your apartment waiting by the phone.

Only Doctors and Hookers Need Pagers

WHAT KIND OF WORLD must we live in when people constantly jump out of their chair every time some device on their body buzzes or rings. Cell phone, pager, BlackBerry, whatever. I have a cell phone—but only in my car. It saves me an hour of doing business in the office. But do people have to walk down the street with a phone on their ear, or an earpiece, talking to no one, like a demented person; or bother everyone in a restaurant, or a movie theater, or a supermarket line, or— can you believe it?—in an elevator with twelve other people forced to listen? Why must the tiny woman in the oversized (but empty) SUV have one hand on the phone and the other on the steering wheel as she negotiates a left turn in heavy traffic? I understand parents want to be available to the nanny, and be reachable in school emergencies, but otherwise, who needs to be instantly accessible? If I call someone and he's not around I'm happy to leave a message.

Cell phones have gotten out of hand. I believe it's mostly an anti-loneliness device. They're today's boom box. Thank goodness cell phones are now banned in health club locker rooms. (With those new camera phones out, I don't want anyone seeing impromptu shots of my naked old ass), and at most private golf courses and some restaurants. No more being in a beautiful setting, lining up a putt, and hearing, "Hello, Manny! Whaddya mean they won't close the deal?!" I hate people who conduct business when the idea of recreation is to recreate. When I complain about this, I hear, "Yeah, but I don't want to miss anything."

I don't need to carry a BlackBerry or a pager, either. Sure, my clients would love to be able to reach me at any moment, but if they could, I'd have no peace. I don't want to be available to people without lives.

Come on. Who *really* needs to be reachable? You're thinking, doctors. Okay. I'd love to have my doctor's cell phone number, but I don't. He's smart; he has a service that pages him, and he knows that nine out of ten times an emergency can be handled easily. The same goes for business.

Here's who *does* need a pager: a hooker. You're horny; she's an impulse buy.

Call me an old fart, but I like a simpler life. I'm not trying to fight the twenty-first century, I'm just looking for a little more civility. To me, personal contact is still the best.

Once, friends in the business used to have lunch for laughs. We do that less now because we're so accessible electronically that by the time anyone gets to lunch there's nothing we don't know about each other. What's left to say? The new world is keeping people from actually getting together, from having fun.

At this very moment, no one knows where to find me—and that's fine with me.

Don't Stiff the Help
and They Won't Stiff You

WHEN I TAKE SOMEONE out for lunch or dinner or to a club, I invariably hear, "Bernie, how did you manage to get the best table?"

My father taught me the basics. He said, "The boss may know you"—he was friends with the owner of the Copacabana in New York, and always got the prime spot in the joint—"but make sure you take care of the maitre d' anyway." I thought that was obvious, but he explained why. "The maitre d' gets hardly any salary; he makes most of his money from tips. He 'owns' these tables. It's the guy's business. By the end of the year it adds up for him, and *you* gain a reputation as a big sport. Certainly you're a guy everyone knows."

The same goes for parking attendants, especially at big hotels. Usually they pay to have the concession. A little knowing wave when you drive up and a well-placed ten-dollar bill will usually ensure that your car is not parked on the back lot and is waiting for you when you come out.

At a restaurant, never duke the maitre d' up-front; that's rude. Slip him a twenty on the way out and he'll take care of you next time. It's less coarse that way. It's like you're really not paying for the table, you're paying for his attention. At some places, five bucks is fine. Just go over, shake his hand, and acknowledge it's the man's table.

I know, some of you are worried that if you don't slip him the twenty up front that you won't get the good table in the first place. Don't worry. A good maitre d' *already* knows who's going to tip him. His eyes (likes those of a pit boss) are all-knowing. The putz who comes in waving a $20 bill will not get the table. It's all about nods. It's an attitude. It's their job to know who's going to give them the money, and who's going to do it without acting like an idiot.

At a neighborhood restaurant, the *owner* is usually also the maitre d'. Him you don't tip. And a good owner will not take it, unless you haven't been in before. When I go someplace new I give the guy a twenty just in case I want to come back.

Occasionally they won't treat you right. I went to a new restaurant in Los Angeles and liked it a lot. I asked the maitre d' her name. She said, "Joan." I told her I was Bernie Brillstein and gave her fifty bucks. The place had only been open three days. A week later I called and asked for Joan. I said, "I'd like a reservation for eight p.m. on Thursday night."

She said, "You can come at six-thirty or ten."

I said, "Is this Joan?"

"Yes."

"This is Bernie Brillstein. Do you remember I was in the other night?"

"No."

I never returned.

But that's where payback should end. Just consider this story: I took my family to Vegas in the late sixties, and went to see one of my management company's clients, the comedian Shelley Berman, at the Fremont. The show went great. The next night, during dinner, I get a call from the Fremont's owner. It seems that at the first show, one of the waitresses dropped a tray in the middle of Shelley's routine. Shelley stopped the show and said to the audience, "You all paid for baby-sitters. You all paid for new gowns. You've all gone to a great deal of trouble to get here tonight. And this woman ruins the show. If I were you, I would not tip the waitresses."

After the show all the waitresses went on strike. I had to run over and talk Shelley into apologizing to the waitresses and promising them that in the second show he'd make a speech on how beautiful they are and how wonderful they are, and to please tip them double.

In Vegas I get free rooms and free food and sometimes comp tickets to prizefights. Is it because they love me? No. I'm a gambler and the hotels want me to lose money. They know the odds: I will probably blow ten times the price of the suite and twenty times the price of the tickets playing craps.

So you'd think I'd put all my tips on the bill.

I don't. I pay cash; it's classier. Even though most hotels

already put the room service gratuity on the bill, I *still* put in an extra five. If I had to bring breakfast to a schmuck like me and I didn't get an extra five, I wouldn't be too thrilled. You've got to give back something for having made it in life.

Besides, I believe that God knows what you're doing all the time. He has the big Merit Book. If you stiff a waiter, he's not the only one who knows it.

You Can Never Get Back from the Future

REMEMBER THE DINNER YOU didn't want to go to, but you couldn't say no so you made the plans? Remember the person you didn't want to see, but you wanted to be polite, so you scheduled a meeting?

Then one day it's, "Oh no, he's coming in."

Don't put off things you don't want to do; just learn to say no right away.

I've said yes instead of no to the dinner, the appointment, to signing a client, to selling a show. Usually I rationalized that I didn't want to hurt someone's feelings. In reality, I did it because in the back of my mind (or maybe the front) I thought I could handle it because I was different from the rest of the putzes. No one is.

My assistant knows this better than anyone. She gets a call from someone who wants to see me. They'll use any excuse. I don't want to do it and won't even get on the phone, but for some reason—say they call in April—I might say, "Give them a time in July." Then I put it out of my mind. The problem is that July always comes and then I'm stuck. No wonder I'm always going, "*Who* is my lunch with?" (Only I don't put it so delicately.) I should have jumped on the phone in the first place and said, "I don't have time for lunch. What do you want?" It only takes five minutes. And most of the people who call you for lunch don't pick up the check anyway.

The problem is that I hate rejection. I always put myself on the other side and think, I'm a big man; I should try to be nice to everyone. But that's my problem. In the end I waste an awful lot of time that way and all I gain is that people are saying what a nice guy I am.

I love that, I admit. But I never feel like such a nice guy when the time comes.

Just Give Me the Gift Bag
and Let Me Go Home

M OST BUSINESS SOCIALIZING IS a big waste of time.

I have never made a business deal at a party. If I have to go, I don't try to sell. I don't network because after a couple drinks who remembers what you said, or even who you are? If you're looking to meet the noodles who don't want to talk to you during the day, what's the sense?

Who ever gets a job at a party? Even if someone knows what you do, he's not thinking about it unless he's trying to get work *from* you. I'd rather not be bothered. It's not the time or the place. A party is just a bunch of people patting each other on the back, saying, "Remember I met you?" It's the same people from the party a week earlier, posing the same way. And the place they met you was at the *last party*. The only good that comes out of a party is when you're young and hoping to get laid. I'm neither.

Usually, I walk in early, get my picture taken with the guest of honor—if it's that kind of party—and walk out the back door carrying the gift bag. No one knows the difference.

You make deals at work.

No wonder the William Morris Agency credo was, "That's why we have offices with our name on them, not restaurants."

Take the famous Monday night at Morton's tradition. Most of those who go don't do it for the food—which is excellent—but to be seen. But if your only purpose is to be seen, and you go to a place that caters to that desire, then you only ever see the people who feel they have to be seen. And the tourists. What good can you do each other besides say, "Oh, you're here, too."

Some die-hards do it every day of the week. There's a guy who has lunch every day at the Grill, in Beverly Hills. He sits at the same table, just to get known. I still don't know what he does. I only know he's always there. "Hello, Mr. Brillstein." He probably thinks that as soon as he's known he'll quit going, but I doubt it. How can he show what's he's got—unless he steals silverware?

Same with after-hours business functions. Tell you the truth, no one I know except people trying to climb the ladder of power and influence like to go. My rule is it that you don't have to be friends with the people you're in business with—and you don't have to pretend. It's okay to be great associates. On your deathbed you'll never say, "I wish I'd gone to one more cocktail party and seen Mike."

Of course, when I was younger there were always places I desperately wanted to be invited. Until I went. The Oscars and Emmys are great—until you lose. Boring. Charity dinners seemed so glamorous. Boring. Here's the truth: Even if you're young, I wouldn't go to these events or places to meet the hottest people because by the time you manage to get in, their heat will probably be gone. Instead, find someone who's been around for a while and is constantly doing good stuff. Take him or her to lunch. Form a relationship. Let that person mentor you.

Another post-workday social function is the fund-raising event. Giving money to worthy charities, I love; going to fund-raising events, I don't. Most of the people who throw these events don't even know how to do it right. Cocktail hour lasts two. The silent auction is a silent yawn. I've already seen the entertainment eight hundred times. I recently attended an event where dinner wasn't served until eleven o'clock! I left.

If I could just send a check I'd give them double.

Carry a Big Stick But Have a Bigger Heart

WHEN YOU ATTAIN A certain lofty power position in business and/or life, people will either be impressed by you or think you're an ass.

Usually you have to be both.

I want what I want, and I've always done everything in my power to get it; but even when I was the thousand-pound gorilla in the room, I was happy to leave something on the table. Money and morality are a tough call, but I just don't believe in killing the people I deal with. Besides, someday I may need *them,* and I don't want them to have been waiting for years for their chance to kill *me.*

The result is a pocket of goodwill. It inevitably comes in handy when things could go either way in a deal, in hiring someone, or in getting the services you want. In a fifty-fifty situation, the perception that you have a heart might be the little edge you need to make matters go your way.

With any luck, the day will come when you have power.

That's when you should stop for a moment and think about how to use it.

For me, there was nothing like building the client list I'd dreamed of and then realizing, in the middle of a party after the Blues Brothers' show at the Universal Amphitheater, packed with movers and shakers, that I'd done it.

Driving to work the next morning, I knew success had happened for me. Waiting at a red light on Sunset Boulevard, I felt like the road was wide open. But, somehow, I also realized that despite now owning the big stick, my struggle should be to have a bigger heart.

If someone was screwing up, I'd tell them immediately— and help them work on their mistakes. Give them a break. Later, if they still couldn't get it right, I'd tell them that, too— and let them move on. I'd be a benevolent despot, always keeping in mind that my employees and coworkers had families and lives and depended on me.

It's not always about the bottom line.

What's the Big Deal?
We're All Going to Die

YOU JOINED THE COMPANY when you were twenty-five and now you're fifty-five. Unless you're in line for the top, there's not much chance of you climbing a lot higher on the corporate ladder. Still, you're a valuable asset and your bosses want to keep you around. Half of you thinks, I've got to keep up, especially with the younger generation. The other half thinks, Just let me do my job until it's over.

What do you do?

Don't separate yourself from young people just because you're "old." Make yourself part of what's going on. I'm seventy-two now and still vital. I don't buy movie tickets at the senior discount, and I still have my sense of humor, except when any woman under thirty-five calls me "Sir." I don't want to be the old guy playing pinochle at a country club, talking to other old people about their operations, their prostates, their medications, their late husbands and wives.

It's easy to be current: Read everything, watch TV, listen to the radio, hang out some—even if it's only in the lunchroom or by the water cooler. So what if everything the young people talk about seems familiar—just with different names and faces—because you've been there before. Okay, so you know that life runs in cycles. What's old is new again. The new generation doesn't; it's still fresh to them, full of energy. Tap that energy.

Tune in to your kids. Don't say, "We didn't do things that way." I told my kids about Tony Bennett; they told me about Eminem. I heard a group called Outkast; they're as good as Earth, Wind, and Fire. I remember when the Rolling Stones were the radicals, but I sometimes listen to rap music. Well, I try.

But don't be a pushover. If you hear something that's obviously bullshit, say so. And tell the kids why. You'll be surprised: They'll listen to you. Just because some kid in your conservative company has long hair and wears jeans with his ass crack showing, that doesn't make him an idiot, just trendy. And naive. Don't dismiss him out of hand because he's sloppy. Teach him to dress appropriate to the role he signed on to play.

Just because you're closer to the end of your career than to the beginning, doesn't mean you have to stop thinking creatively. There's value in the wisdom you've accumulated. Find new ways to make your job better. Save your boss some money.

I've adjusted to my age by working harder, but with ten clients instead of fifty. Age does have some limitations, so I stopped doing so much that I couldn't do anything. Somehow, I've gained enormous respect from the young people around me. They say, "How do you do it?"

Just like always: I bet on what I believe in. Good advice no matter what your age.

These days, I can't say I'm going to run a marathon. Running across the street is a marathon enough. I can't play three sets of tennis in a row, either. I would love it if my legs had held up, but they always say the legs are the first to go. In my case something else went first, but that's neither here nor there. At least it wasn't my brain.

Someone Up There Is Watching

THESE DAYS I THINK about retiring more than I ever did. I started the process a few years ago when I sold my half of the company to my partner. I had no illusions about what it meant. I was no longer king. It took me some time to get used to it. A doctor does it by bringing in some associates, then he cuts his schedule to two days a week, then to no days. He might think he's still king—his name is on the practice—but he's not; you have to be there to be king. This goes for the delicatessen owner, the sporting goods salesman, anyone.

I had to learn to accept it. We all do, eventually.

Funny, but letting go of some of my responsibilities made me want to do anything but retire. Suddenly I had more clients than ever, and I was having fun.

Still, I know I have to prepare myself for the day I finally walk out the door. When I go I want to go out on my own terms, and I want to leave behind a legacy I can respect. I'm in my seventies and I still work at it every day. So far, I figure I'm okay unless I do something schmucky in the next twenty years.

By the way, why wait to think about this? It's never too early to start.

Reputation is built by the steadiness of doing the same thing all the time, and doing it well. Being honest. Not toying with people's lives. Having people respect what you say. Don't hurt people's feelings on purpose. Try to bring laughter to the world. And love. You still have to back that up with actions, though, or people will think you're full of it.

One way I stay straight is to have sources for the truth. These are trusted people I can talk with when I'm not sure about a situation or how to proceed. My wife, Carrie. Close friends, some clients. I used to use my father because he was a very basic, truthful guy. Too bad he's gone.

Another way to stay on the right track is to acknowledge that God is watching. It's a pragmatic thing: We all have our jobs to do, and I guess someone *has* to be God. The God of everyone. He lives on a cloud; he's all-seeing and all-knowing. I think God is even watching me write this now, and he's saying, "I hope you're not going to be a putz, kid."

God has the book on each person in front of him. He knows if we do good things or bad. He knows if you stiff a waiter. He knows if you ever hurt anyone intentionally. He knows if you treat people graciously, spread money around if you can, and try not to cause hardship.

When it's my time to go, he—okay, he could be a she—will review the check marks. At this point I like to think I'm ahead of the game and there will be some reward, but I confess that I don't really know what happens after you die. My father is gone and if he were sitting up there having a party he'd have called me by now.

Believing in something greater than ourselves is what it takes to put us in our place. Otherwise our egos would be out of control. I believe that 100 percent. You've got to believe in something other than money or sports or a good movie. The other night, my wife and I were in bed. I was very tired. The dog came up on the bed and wrapped himself around my neck. My wife, the dog, and I were lying there, and it felt so damn good that I'd pay a million dollars for more moments like that. I know it sounds sappy, but I believe God gave that to me, and if I watch my step, I may get more.

I don't think I was conscious of my legacy until recently. I thought more about making a living than what I'd leave behind. But when the idea of how you'll be remembered hits you, it hits you for good.

Now that I've sold the company to Brad Grey, and he gets to be king, the guy who says yes or no, I have more time to consider what I'm leaving behind. And speaking of leaving, this much I know: I don't want to have a heart attack in the office. I don't want people to say, "He died at his desk. Isn't that great?"

As I once told Larry King, when I'm finally gone, at least I know what I want on my gravestone. Once I wanted it to read: "From *Hee Haw* to *Saturday Night Live* to *Dangerous Liaisons*," but it's gone far beyond that now.

So maybe this:

He made a difference. He made people laugh.
He made people happy. People wanted to be with him.
Not now, though.

Acknowledgments

Bernie:

Thanks to Brad Grey, Christina Berger, Peter Safran, Kassie Evashevski, and everyone at Brillstein-Grey; Brian DeFiore and Kate Garrick at DeFiore and Company; Bill Shinker, Lauren Marino, Hilary Terrell, and everyone at Gotham Books; Marcy Engelman; David Sipress; the late Wallace S. Jordan; and David Rensin, who always gets my voice, and more important, gets my act.

◆

David:

Thanks to everyone in my corner—you know who you are—particularly Cynthia Price and Bill Zehme; to Bernie for always watching over me; and especially to my wife, Suzie Peterson, and son, Emmett Rensin, for their love, patience, support, and joy in life that makes everything I do worth doing.

About the Authors

BERNIE BRILLSTEIN is the founding partner of Brillstein-Grey Entertainment, the most powerful management/production company in Hollywood, whose clients include Brad Pitt, Jennifer Aniston, Adam Sandler, and Dennis Miller. Bernie's current personal clients include Rob Lowe, Wayne Brady, Martin Short, and Lorne Michaels. During his career, Bernie has also represented Jim Henson, John Belushi, Gilda Radner, and many others. He is the author, with David Rensin, of *Where Did I Go Right?: You're No One in Hollywood Unless Someone Wants You Dead*. He lives in Beverly Hills.

◆

DAVID RENSIN has coauthored eleven books and five *New York Times* bestsellers, including Chris Rock's *Rock This!* and Tim Allen's *Don't Stand Too Close to a Naked Man*. He lives in Los Angeles.